"The best kids' books are the ones that are equally beloved by adults. *New Favorites for New Cooks* is one of those: essential in your kitchen however young, or old, you are. Carolyn Federman's enthusiasm gets even an old cook like me making hand-pressed tortillas and baking homemade honey-cinnamon granola!"

—CAL PETERNELL, author of *Twelve Recipes* and *A Recipe for Cooking*

"Carolyn Federman knows as well as I do that if you introduce kids to real food and teach them in the garden, at farmers' markets, and in the kitchen, they will want to cook and eat every kind of food. Wisely, she has chosen the most simple yet delicious recipes based on fresh, whole produce in season. But most importantly, she has shown kids that they are capable of anything."

—ALICE WATERS, owner of Chez Panisse and founder of The Edible Schoolyard Project

NEW FAVORITES for NEW COOKS

NEW FAVORITES
for NEW COOKS

50 delicious recipes for kids to make

Carolyn Federman

photographs by Aubrie Pick

TEN SPEED PRESS
California | New York

CONTENTS

Introduction 1

chapter 1
FAVORITE BREAKFAST 11

chapter 2
ANYTIME LUNCH 35

chapter 3
IN-BETWEEN MEALS AND AFTER-SCHOOL SNACKS 69

chapter 4
SOMETHING TO DRINK 95

chapter 5
WHAT'S FOR DINNER? 119

chapter 6
SWEETS AND TREATS 141

Tools (That You Will Need to Use This Book) 159
Glossary of Cooking Terms 163
Acknowledgments 166
Index 167

Not what we have
but what we enjoy,
constitutes our abundance.

—EPICURUS

Have patience. All things
are difficult before they
become easy.

—SAADI SHIRAZI

INTRODUCTION

A cookbook can be a tool and a treasure for life. The recipes become like old friends, the pages stained with every masterpiece and all the disasters, too. I learned how to use a cookbook through lots of trial and error. The most important things I learned can be boiled down to three directions.

1. Read the whole recipe before getting started.
2. If a word or ingredient is unfamiliar, look it up.
3. It's supposed to be fun, so don't worry so much about getting it "right."

You may find that even if you read through the whole recipe, look up all the new words, and prepare everything just the way it says, the dish still doesn't exactly work out. You are not alone. I can count on one hand the number of recipes that turned out right the first time I made them. And I have been cooking every day for more than twenty years!

And what about those photos? Is all food supposed to look that "perfect"?

Actually, no! The photographs in these pages are here to inspire you, not to scare you off. I spent many days with a professional photographer and food stylist—someone whose job is to arrange and rearrange the food so that it looks as tempting as can be! If you put a lot of heart into your cooking, your food will be even lovelier—and yummier—than pictures can convey.

When you make something over and over, it becomes so familiar that you may not even need the recipe to make it the next time. Then it becomes part of your repertoire—a sort of cookbook in your head that you can access easily and often. My hope is that, by using this book again and again, you will begin to build or expand your own cooking repertoire.

HEY PARENTS, TAKE SAFETY SERIOUSLY IN THE KITCHEN!

* Review knife skills with your kids (see page 7).

* Teach new cooks to always use oven mitts when handling hot dishes, and to stir and taste hot things with long-handled spoons.

* If they are using appliances or knives for the first time, make the recipe *with* them and demonstrate how to safely use these tools.

* Remind them again and again, until it becomes second nature, to turn off the stove and other appliances when the food has finished cooking.

* Show them how to wash produce, and to be vigilant about washing hands before getting started.

* Use the following Recipe Rating System to decide if they can manage a recipe independently or if they will need your hands-on supervision.

* Insist they clean up—it's an integral part of the job for every professional chef! That said, kids will gain more confidence in the kitchen if you give in to the mess along the way.

RECIPE RATING SYSTEM

These icons indicate what to look out for in the recipe.

 Cutting, trimming, or chopping is needed. Get an adult to help if you haven't used a knife before.

 This recipe uses heat—oven or stove.

 Caution! Hot oil.

GETTING STARTED IN THE KITCHEN

A little preparation goes a long way to making great food. These are a few simple (really!) ways to make your time in the kitchen easier and more fun.

prepare

* **Read the recipe in advance.** It's really disappointing to get halfway through a recipe and find out it needs to chill overnight.

* **Check your pantry.** Do you have what you need? If not, make a shopping list for your family's next trip to the grocery store. Do you have the tools needed? Or items that can work in their place?

* **Wash your hands, and wash fresh produce.** Do this before you get started. Recipes don't usually mention this, which means the author assumes it has been done.

take care

* **Follow the recipe in order.** If not, there's a good chance the recipe won't quite work out.

* **Clean up as you go.** While the water is coming to a boil, the oven is preheating, or the vegetables are roasting, take a moment to tidy up. Use a bowl to collect scraps, and then deposit them into the compost when you're done with prep. Keeping things clean along the way keeps the after-cooking cleanup time short and sweet.

* **Be patient and keep at it.** *Every* cook, from amateur to professional, makes mistakes, lots and lots of them!

investigate

* **Use the glossary and the Internet!** Getting to know the language of recipes will give you a good head start for making great food. Terms in **boldface** are defined in the glossary. Each time you come across a new term, take a moment to look it up. The next time you see it, you'll know exactly what it means.

Ask for help. If you've never used a knife before, or you're not sure how to set the timer on the oven, ask an adult. Chances are your questions will have quick and simple answers.

Use all of your senses. Smell, see, hear, touch, and taste the food as you prepare it. Tasting is especially important after stirring in salt, spices, oil, or vinegar so that you can adjust the flavor along the way.

WHAT'S IN YOUR PANTRY?

Check your spice shelf. Have those jars been there for, like, six years? Open the container and use your power of smell. If they don't smell good, they won't taste good either.

Oil doesn't last forever! After a time, and particularly after exposure to heat, the good fats in oil break down, spoiling the flavor. This rancid (spoiled) oil has a fishy, unpleasant smell and can ruin the flavor of your food. Different oils have different flavors, too, so taste the oil to make sure you like it. I like olive oil best, and I choose one that is mild, not spicy, so it doesn't overpower my food.

A note about salt. The amount of salt in these recipes is based on *coarse* salt, because that's what I use in my kitchen. Coarse salts, like kosher or coarse sea salt, have a slightly larger grain and, in my opinion, a nicer flavor than table salt.

Everything has a season. Produce tastes best when it is at the peak of its season—think of a juicy late-summer peach, or fresh, tender spring peas. If that peach is in the market in December, you can bet it comes from far away (maybe another continent). It was picked too early, still green, so it could survive the long trip to the grocery store. This can make for a bland, mealy peach, or worse, one that rots before it ripens. Look for fruit that is soft but not mushy (overripe!) and is heavy with juice, and choose vegetables that are firm and crisp, not limp or rubbery, and small to medium in size, not extra-large.

A Quick Guide to Measuring and Measurements

We use different equipment to measure liquid and dry ingredients because, even though the measures hold the same amount, the way we use them is different.

* **For dry ingredients, use a plastic or metal measuring cup or spoon.** Fill the cup/spoon with the ingredient, then scrape a butter knife across the top to brush off the excess. This is called the "scoop and sweep" method.

* **For liquids, use a clear (glass or plastic) measure.** Look for the line that corresponds to the amount listed in the recipe. Hold up the measuring cup to eye level, or bend down to countertop level, so you can see the liquid lining up with the correct measurement.

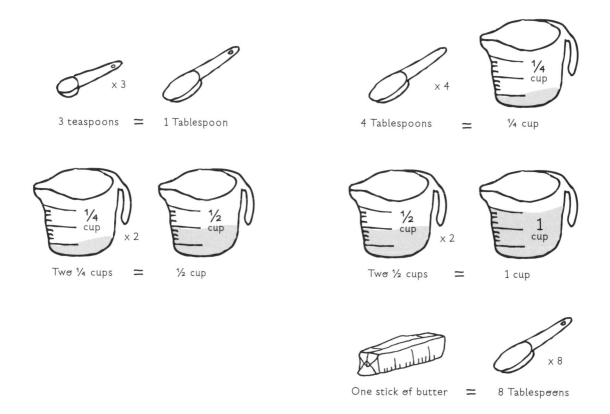

3 teaspoons   =   1 Tablespoon   4 Tablespoons   =   ¼ cup

Two ¼ cups   =   ½ cup   Two ½ cups   =   1 cup

One stick of butter   =   8 Tablespoons

The Most Important Tool in the Kitchen:
A KNIFE SKILLS PRIMER

Just like with any other tool, you have to first learn how to use a knife, and then your "knife skills" will get better as you practice. I know you already know this, but just in case . . . always hold a knife by the handle! If you've never used knives for cooking, ask an adult to try it with you the first few times. Learn these *three key hand gestures* to keep your fingers protected. Most important, *keep your eyes on what you're doing, and take it slow.*

See how the fingertips are tucked and protected from the sharp blade? That's "the claw"!

1.
The Claw
Make a claw to protect your fingertips. Use your fingertips to hold the produce in place.

2.
The Claw and Saw
Hold the produce in place with "the claw." Move the knife back and forth in a sawing motion. Move your fingertips back a little bit after each cut to keep space between your fingers and the blade.

3.
The Tunnel and Saw
Hold the produce with the fingertips of one hand arched over the produce to make a tunnel. Place the knife in the tunnel and cut with a sawing motion.

KNIFE TECHNIQUES

You'll find these basic methods of preparing food throughout this book, and in just about *every* cookbook, so they are good terms to know by heart. Start by creating a flat edge on the produce—cutting it in half, and half again, to make a fruit or vegetable more manageable to work with.

Chop To cut into uneven pieces. To *coarsely chop* makes more or less bite-size pieces; *finely chopped* means roughly ⅛-inch to ¼-inch pieces, about the size of a ladybug.

Chiffonade To slice into thin strips, or "ribbons." Most often for herbs such as basil or mint for a **garnish**. To chiffonade, stack the herb leaves, roll them into a pencil shape, and thinly slice them **crosswise**.

Dice To cut into cubes, anywhere from ⅛ inch to ½ inch. *Diced* food is meant to be uniform in size and shape. Here are some real-life size references:

- ⅛ inch looks like an ant
- ¼ inch looks like a ladybug
- ½ inch looks like a piece of popcorn
- 1 inch looks like an almond

Julienne To cut into sticks—either small (like matchsticks) or large (like french fries).

Mince To cut into teeny-tiny pieces, about the size of ants (the littlest ones). Mincing is even smaller than finely chopped.

Types of Knives

chef's knife

paring knife

serrated knife

Chiffonade

Mince

Dice

Julienne

Chop

CHAPTER 1

FAVORITE BREAKFAST

Fruit and Yogurt Parfaits 13

Blueberry-Lemon Scones 14

Sweet and Simple Breakfast Toppers: Strawberry Sauce,
Apricot Quick Jam, and Homemade Butter 16

Honey-Cinnamon Granola 21

Brown Sugar Polenta 22

Ham and Egg Breakfast Sandwich 24

Pioneer Pancakes 27

Silver Dollar Johnnycakes 29

Cheddar Cheese Frittata 30

Never work before eating breakfast. If you have to work before breakfast, eat your breakfast first.

—JOSH BILLINGS
(AKA HENRY WHEELER SHAW)

FRUIT AND YOGURT PARFAITS

You might have everything you need to make this dessert-y breakfast right now. What are you waiting for? A parfait is made with layers and served in a tall glass so you can see all of the ingredients at once. Parfait works with any combination of fruit, so substitute your favorites in any season. The fruit can be fresh or cooked, but I like to cook blueberries because it brings out their flavor tenfold. Plus, it makes great purple streaks in the yogurt.

you will need

Measuring cups, measuring spoons, small saucepan, 6 to 8 small clear glasses or cups (small mason jars will also work)

ingredients

2 cups berries (blueberries, blackberries, raspberries, boysenberries, or a combination)

2 tablespoons water

2 teaspoons sugar

1 cup plain whole-milk yogurt

preparation

1 In a small saucepan over medium-high heat, combine the berries, water, and sugar and bring to a gentle **simmer**. Turn the heat to medium-low and stir constantly for 2 to 3 minutes, or until the fruit is soft and the juice starts to thicken into a syrup. Remove the pan from the heat, and turn off the stove. Let cool for 2 to 3 minutes.

2 Spoon 1 tablespoon of the yogurt into each small glass and then top with 1 tablespoon of the cooked berries. Repeat alternating layers of fruit and yogurt for a total of four layers, or a few more!

3 Parfaits are best eaten right away, but they can rest, covered, in the refrigerator for up to 1 hour if needed.

VARIATION

Add 1 tablespoon of granola (see page 21) between each layer of yogurt.

BLUEBERRY-LEMON SCONES

These scones are easy-peasy lemon-breezy for a weekend breakfast treat or snack. I especially love how the whole-wheat flour gives them an oh-so-much-more-than-a-scone feel in every bite. I don't mind a few squished blueberries in my scones; but if you want them to stay perfectly round, put them in the freezer for up to 10 minutes (but no longer!) and take them out just before mixing them into the dough. These scones are delicious served with a cup of tea or a glass of milk.

you will need

Measuring cups, measuring spoons, baking sheet, parchment paper, citrus zester or small grater, large bowl, whisk

ingredients

2 cups whole-wheat flour, plus a few pinches for dusting the cutting board

1 lemon

2½ teaspoons baking powder

¾ teaspoon coarse salt

⅓ cup sugar, plus 1 tablespoon

1½ cups heavy whipping cream, plus 1 tablespoon

1 cup fresh or frozen blueberries, rinsed and dried (see Note)

preparation

1 Preheat the oven to 400°F. Line a baking sheet with parchment paper and **dust** a cutting board with flour.

2 Using a citrus zester, **zest** the lemon by finely grating just the yellow skin (not the white **pith** between skin and fruit).

3 In a large bowl, whisk together the flour, baking powder, salt, ⅓ cup sugar, and lemon zest. Whisk from the bottom to mix everything in.

4 Add the 1½ cups cream to the flour mixture and stir with your hands to bring the dough together. It won't be a perfectly smooth ball—more like a misshapen lump. (It's okay if bits of dough stick to your fingers, but if your hands are covered, **knead** in another 1 to 2 teaspoons flour.)

5 Sprinkle the dough with the blueberries and push and pull gently with your hands to mix them in. It's okay if some of the blueberries get smashed.

6 Move the dough to the floured cutting board and form it into a disc, about 1 inch high and 8 inches across. With the tip of your finger, spread the remaining 1 tablespoon cream over the top of the dough and then sprinkle with the remaining 1 tablespoon sugar. Cut the round into eight equal wedges and arrange them, without crowding, on the prepared baking sheet.

7 **Bake** for 15 to 20 minutes, or until lightly browned. Turn off the oven, remove the scones, and let cool for 2 minutes before serving.

SWEET AND SIMPLE BREAKFAST TOPPERS

What could be better than pancakes with maple syrup or hot buttered toast with jam? How about pancakes drizzled with homemade strawberry sauce or toast topped with butter and jam that you make yourself?

STRAWBERRY SAUCE

Makes about ½ cup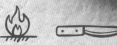

you will need

Measuring cup, measuring spoons, paring knife, small saucepan, wooden spoon

ingredients

1 pint ripe strawberries

¼ cup water

3 to 4 tablespoons sugar (see Note)

A tiny **pinch** of coarse salt

preparation

1 With a paring knife, hull (remove the green stems and leaves from) the strawberries and slice the berries **lengthwise**, from the **stem end** down, roughly ⅛ inch thick (about the thickness of a quarter).

2 In a small saucepan, stir together the sliced strawberries, water, and 3 tablespoons of the sugar with a wooden spoon.

3 Bring to a **simmer** over medium-high heat. Stir in the salt, turn the heat to medium-low, and cook, uncovered, for about 10 minutes. Turn off the stove.

4 There should be some slices still intact, surrounded by a syrupy sauce. You can leave the slices whole, or, if you like, break up bigger pieces with the back of the spoon.

5 Strawberry sauce will keep, in an **airtight** container, in the refrigerator for up to 3 days.

NOTE

The sweetness of strawberries can vary a lot. Before removing the syrup from the stove, taste it—carefully, it will be very hot!—and add more sugar by the teaspoon if needed.

DID YOU KNOW?

Strawberries absorb more pesticides than nearly any other produce. So when you choose organic strawberries, which are grown without pesticides, you are doing a good turn for yourself and the planet.

APRICOT QUICK JAM

Makes about 1½ cups

you will need

Measuring cup, measuring spoons, paring knife, small saucepan, wooden spoon, clean glass jar big enough to hold 1 cup liquid

ingredients

1 pound ripe apricots (see Note)

¾ cup plus 2 tablespoons sugar

2 tablespoons water

preparation

1 Remove the stems from the apricots, then, cut or pull the apricots in half and remove the pits. (There's no need to peel them.)

2 In a small saucepan, combine the apricots, sugar, and water. Place over high heat and cook, stirring, until the sugar is completely wet and the mixture is gently simmering—a minute or two.

3 Turn the heat to medium and cook, uncovered, for 8 to 10 minutes, stirring occasionally with a wooden spoon. For a smoother jam, cook up to 5 minutes longer. The apricots will be soft and broken up and the skin more or less dissolved. They should have the consistency of a sauce. If you like, break up bigger chunks by mashing them with the back of the wooden spoon. Turn off the stove and let the jam cool.

4 Once the jam has cooled to room temperature, transfer to a clean jar with a tightly fitted lid. Quick jam will thicken as it cools, so if it's a little too sauce-like, refrigerate for about 30 minutes. The jam will keep in the refrigerator for up to 5 days.

NOTE

Like other fruit, the sweetness of apricots can vary. Taste the jam—carefully, it will be very hot!—and add sugar by the teaspoon if needed. Cook in the additional sugar over low heat and taste as you go to make sure the flavor is balanced.

HOMEMADE BUTTER

Makes about ½ cup

you will need

Measuring cup, 12-ounce glass jar with an **airtight** lid, fine-mesh strainer or cheesecloth, storage container or small bowl

ingredients

½ cup heavy whipping cream

preparation

1 Pour the cream into a jar and close the lid. Shake the jar quickly for 5 minutes, or until a solid mass begins to form, then shake it for 1 minute longer. The cream will start to come away from the sides of the jar. The sound will change to sloshing as solid butter begins to form and separate from the liquid.

2 **Strain** through a fine-mesh strainer or cheesecloth to remove any extra liquid and then transfer the butter to a storage container.

3 Fresh butter will keep, tightly covered, in the refrigerator for up to 3 days.

FLAVORED BUTTERS, 1-2-3

For **maple butter**: Use a fork to **whip** 1 tablespoon maple syrup or honey and ⅛ teaspoon salt into the freshly strained butter.

For **brown sugar butter**: Use a rubber spatula or a fork to beat ¼ cup plus 1 tablespoon light brown sugar into the freshly strained butter until the sugar has dissolved.

For **herb butter**: Finely **chop** the leaves of 1 sprig thyme and 1 sprig marjoram until you have ½ teaspoon of each. (Remember to use "the claw" to protect your fingers.) Use a fork to mash the herbs and ⅛ teaspoon salt into the freshly strained butter.

Try granola on top
of yogurt with honey
and blueberries!

HONEY-CINNAMON GRANOLA

Granola is great to make in big batches, so you can have it to eat all week long. It makes an easy breakfast—more filling than cereal—and a perfect after-school snack. Add it to a bowl of yogurt, top it with milk and fruit, or mix it with chocolate chips and roasted nuts for an afternoon pick-me-up.

you will need

Measuring cups, measuring spoons, baking sheet, parchment paper, large bowl, small saucepan, wooden spoon

ingredients

4 cups rolled (old-fashioned) oats

1 tablespoon plus 1 teaspoon brown sugar

1 teaspoon ground cinnamon

A **pinch** of salt

¼ cup coconut oil or sunflower oil

½ cup honey

½ cup roasted, salted pumpkin seeds

½ cup roasted, salted sunflower seeds

½ cup roasted sesame seeds (optional)

½ cup dried fruit (such as cranberries or raisins)

Milk or yogurt and chopped fruit for serving

preparation

1 Preheat the oven to 325°F. Line a baking sheet with parchment paper.

2 In a large bowl, toss together the oats, brown sugar, cinnamon, and salt.

3 In a small saucepan over low heat, melt the coconut oil. Once melted, measure to be sure you have ¼ cup. (Melt more oil if needed.) Return the coconut oil to the saucepan, add the honey, and warm until combined, about 1 minute, stirring once or twice with a wooden spoon. Turn off the stove and then pour the honey mixture over the oat mixture. Stir well with the spoon and then spread the oat mixture onto the prepared baking sheet in one layer.

4 **Bake** for 25 to 30 minutes, until crisp and lightly browned. Check after 15 minutes if you prefer it lightly toasted. Remove from the oven (don't forget to turn off the oven) and immediately sprinkle the pumpkin seeds, sunflower seeds, sesame seeds (if using), and dried fruit over the top. Let the granola cool for 10 minutes, then remove it from the parchment and break it up into small chunks.

5 Serve in a bowl topped with milk or yogurt and chopped fruit. Granola may be stored in a jar with a tightly fitting lid, at room temperature, for up to 1 month.

BROWN SUGAR POLENTA

Polenta is a type of cornmeal that thickens into a creamy porridge—thick and sweet like corn pudding—when cooked with milk and butter. Topped with brown sugar, this is my favorite way to warm things up on a chilly winter morning.

you will need

Measuring cups, measuring spoons, large pot, wooden spoon

ingredients

2 to 2¼ cups milk, plus a splash for serving

2 cups water

1 teaspoon coarse salt

1 cup dried polenta (not instant)

¼ cup **packed** light brown sugar, plus more for serving

2 tablespoons unsalted butter

preparation

1 In a large pot (a Dutch oven or stockpot works well), combine 2 cups of the milk, the water, and ½ teaspoon of the salt. Place over medium-high heat and bring to a **boil**.

2 When the mixture comes to a boil, pour in the polenta slowly, about ¼ cup at a time, stirring constantly with a long-handled wooden spoon until the polenta is well combined with the milk. Break up any lumps with the spoon.

3 Turn the heat to medium-low and gently **simmer** for 20 minutes. Give the polenta a stir every few minutes. If it's sticking to the pan, lower the heat. To test for doneness, taste a small (cooled!) spoonful. It should be creamy, not gritty. If it's not creamy, add another ¼ cup milk and simmer for another 5 to 10 minutes.

4 Turn off the stove and then stir in the brown sugar, butter, and remaining ½ teaspoon salt.

5 Serve hot with a splash of milk and another sprinkle of brown sugar **to taste**.

TIP

If the heat is too high, hot bits of polenta
sometimes jump out of the pot, so be sure to use
a long-handled spoon, and lower the heat a little
if the polenta seems to be erupting like a volcano.

HAM AND EGG BREAKFAST SANDWICH

Nothing beats the comfort of this warm and melty meal, no matter what time of day or night. We discovered how much we loved fried-egg sandwiches when we came home from vacation and the only food in the refrigerator was eggs and bread. Go figure! Since then, this has been our "back from vacation" meal—a deliciously dependable reminder that it is oh so good to be home. Try it as is, or up your game with one of the variations. The recipe makes one sandwich, so if you are planning on company, double it.

you will need

Measuring spoons, butter knife, large sauté pan, spatula, small bowl, small spoon

ingredients

1 brioche bun, sliced in half, or 2 slices rustic bread

1½ tablespoons unsalted butter, plus more for the bread

About 2 ounces thinly sliced sharp Cheddar cheese (enough to cover the bread)

1 thick slice or 2 thin slices ham

1 egg

A **pinch** of coarse salt

A pinch of ground black pepper

preparation

1   If using sliced bread, butter the slices on both sides.

2   Warm a large sauté pan over medium-high heat. Add ½ tablespoon of the butter to the pan, put the bun or bread in the pan, turn the heat to high, and cook until the bread starts to brown—a minute or less. To check the bread, lift the edge with a spatula. If it's golden brown, it's ready. Flip the bread over with the spatula and count to 25, then move it to a plate. While the toast is still warm, arrange the cheese slices over one slice, in an even layer.

3   Add the ham to the pan over medium-high heat and cook until it starts to brown a little at the edges—just a few seconds. Flip the ham over and count to 10, then move it from the pan to the toast.

4   Crack the egg into a small bowl and remove any shell pieces with a spoon. Add the remaining 1 tablespoon butter to the pan. Pour the egg into the pool of butter, turn the heat to low, and cook for about 2 minutes, until the egg white is **set** (firm) and changes from translucent (clear) to white.

5   Flip the egg over with the spatula to cook the other side. For a loose yolk, count to 15. For a firm yolk, count to 30. Move the egg onto the bread with the cheese. Sprinkle with the salt and pepper, cover with the other slice of bread, and serve warm. Don't forget to turn off the stove.

VARIATIONS

Spice it up: Just before serving, sprinkle the egg with red pepper flakes, a pinch of cayenne pepper, or a **dash** of Tabasco sauce.

With herbs: Coarsely **chop** fresh herbs (like basil or parsley; remember to use "the claw" to protect your fingers) and sprinkle 1 tablespoon over the egg just before serving.

PIONEER PANCAKES

If you haven't made your own pancakes, you will be surprised and delighted at how easy it is, and if you're a pancake pro, these thin and crispy cakes with their roots on the pioneer trail will be a welcome addition to your recipe box.

you will need

Measuring cups, measuring spoons, large bowl, whisk, small saucepan, small bowl, fork, griddle or frying pan, spatula

ingredients

1 cup buckwheat flour

½ cup all-purpose flour

2 tablespoons sugar

1 tablespoon baking powder

¾ teaspoon coarse salt

¼ cup unsalted butter, plus more for greasing the griddle

1½ cups milk

1 egg

Syrup and/or fruit for serving (optional)

preparation

1 In a large bowl, whisk together the dry ingredients—buckwheat flour, all-purpose flour, sugar, baking powder, and salt.

2 In a small pan over low heat, melt the ¼ cup butter. Put the milk and egg in a small bowl and **blend** them together with a fork. Add the melted butter to the egg-milk mixture and **whip** them with the fork just until they're mixed together.

3 Add the wet ingredients to the dry ingredients. Mix with the fork until there are no dry ingredients at the bottom or sides of the bowl. The batter should be the thickness of a melted milk shake—pourable but not watery.

4 Warm a griddle or frying pan over medium to high heat. To test the heat, drop a bead of water onto the griddle; if it sizzles and evaporates (disappears) immediately, the griddle is ready. Melt 1 teaspoon (a thin slice) butter across the griddle. Starting with three or four pancakes at a time, pour ¼ cup batter onto the griddle for each one, leaving about 1 inch of space between them.

5 When air bubbles appear on top of the pancakes, use a spatula to flip them over and cook for another 2 minutes. The pancakes should be lightly browned on the bottom. Stack them on a plate, add a little more butter to the griddle, and start the next batch. When all the pancakes are cooked, turn off the stove.

6 Serve the pancakes right away while they're warm, topped with syrup or fruit, or both.

Try these with honey
drizzled on top—yum!

SILVER DOLLAR JOHNNYCAKES

Johnnycakes are a buttery and **savory** surprise. Shaped like a regular pancake, but not quite as sweet, they are yum-a-licious with syrup and even better with a slab of butter and a **pinch** of salt alongside eggs, meat, or fish. Johnnycakes, also known as journeycakes, Shawnee cakes, hoecakes, corn pone, and Janiken (say that ten times fast!), were a staple of Native Americans, and this surefire recipe has hardly changed over the years.

you will need

Measuring cups, measuring spoons, medium bowl, small saucepan, small spoon, fork, griddle or skillet, spatula

ingredients

1 cup medium-ground cornmeal

1 tablespoon sugar

1 teaspoon coarse salt

1 cup milk

2 tablespoons unsalted butter, plus more for the griddle

1 egg

Honey, syrup, jam, or fresh fruit for topping

preparation

1 In a medium bowl, combine the cornmeal, sugar, and salt and stir to mix.

2 In a small saucepan over medium-high heat, combine the milk and 2 tablespoons butter and warm until the butter melts and the milk begins to **simmer**, about 3 minutes. When the milk becomes **frothy** (lots of foamy bubbles), take the pan off the stove.

3 Pour the milk over the cornmeal and mix until all the cornmeal is wet. Set it aside for 10 minutes, so the cornmeal soaks in more of the milk.

4 Meanwhile, crack the egg into a small bowl and remove any shell with a spoon. Beat lightly with a fork to break up the yolk. When the cornmeal has rested (all the milk should be absorbed), add the whisked egg and mix well. The batter will be quite liquid-y, not thick like normal pancakes.

5 Warm a griddle or skillet to medium-high and **grease** with a dab (1 teaspoon or so) of butter. When the butter sizzles, pour the batter, 2 tablespoons at a time, onto the griddle and cook for 1 to 2 minutes. When small bubbles appear on the sides and top of the cakes, flip each one over with a spatula and cook for another 2 minutes. The sides should be crispy and the cakes well browned. Stack the cakes on a plate as they finish cooking, and cover with a clean kitchen towel until they are all done. Turn off the griddle.

6 Top the johnnycakes with honey, syrup, jam, or fresh fruit and eat immediately!

CHEDDAR CHEESE FRITTATA

Frittata (fri-ta-ta) is basically Italian for "baked omelet," and it can mean anything from plain Jane to gussied up, thin and flat to fat and fluffy. This one is light and tasty, and the quick-cooking spinach makes it a guest-worthy meal that's ready in minutes. With a simple base of eggs and cheese, a frittata can handle just about any filling you dream up. Serve it with toasted baguette for breakfast or with a little green salad for lunch.

you will need

Measuring cups, measuring spoons, large bowl, medium bowl, small spoon, whisk, 8-inch ovenproof skillet, oven mitt, knife, spatula

ingredients

1 bunch fresh spinach (about 3 cups of leaves, loosely **packed**)

1 garlic clove

4 eggs

Coarse salt

Ground black pepper

About ¼ cup grated Cheddar or Monterey Jack cheese (see Note)

2 tablespoons olive oil

preparation

1 Preheat the broiler.

2 Fill a large bowl with cool water. Using a knife, trim the stems from the spinach and wash the leaves *thoroughly* by dunking them into the water and stirring with your hands. **Drain** the water and any dirt at the bottom of the bowl, and rinse the spinach again. Drain well. Coarsely **chop** the spinach (just enough to cut the leaves in half or quarters; remember to use "the claw" to protect your fingers). Peel and **mince** the garlic (see page 8).

3 In a medium bowl, crack the eggs, remove any shell with a spoon, and whisk in ⅛ teaspoon salt, a **pinch** of ground pepper, and the cheese.

4 Put 1 tablespoon of the olive oil in an 8-inch **ovenproof** skillet and place over medium heat. Count to 15. Add the garlic and a pinch of salt and stir a few times until the garlic is fragrant.

5 Add the spinach to the pan all at once and cook, stirring, until it is soft and wilted, about 2 minutes.

CONTINUED

VARIATIONS

All sorts of ingredients go with a frittata,
so feel free to experiment. Cook the additions first,
add them to the pan, then add the eggs according to
the main recipe. In the summer, try it with fresh chopped
tomatoes and herbs; in winter, use potatoes with chives and
Cheddar cheese. The possibilities are really truly endless.

6 Add the remaining 1 tablespoon olive oil to the pan and stir so the spinach and oil coat the bottom of the pan. Pour in the eggs and tilt the pan—holding it by the handle—so the bottom is covered by eggs. Cook, without stirring, until the eggs just begin to get firm, about 1 minute. Turn off the stove.

7 Use an oven mitt to transfer the pan to the oven. Cook under the broiler for 2 minutes, or until the eggs are just **set** (they don't wiggle when you move the pan from side to side). Don't cook them longer than 3 minutes, even if they look a little loose—they will continue to cook when they come out of the oven and will turn rubbery and dry if they overcook. Use the oven mitt to take the pan out of the oven, and turn off the oven.

8 Slide a butter knife around the inside edge of the pan to loosen the frittata, cut the frittata into wedges, and use a spatula to dish it onto plates. Eat right away, while it's still warm, or let cool to room temperature.

NOTE

Any mild, meltable cheese, such as Swiss, feta, or crumbled goat cheese, will work.

HOW TO CRACK AN EGG

1.
Hold it in one hand and gently but firmly smack it against the edge of the bowl.

2.
Slip the egg over the least jagged part of the shell, into the bowl. The jagged edges can pop the yolk.

TIP

Use one half of the eggshell or a spoon to scoop out any bits of shell.

> When people you greatly admire appear to be thinking deep thoughts, they probably are thinking about lunch.
>
> —DOUGLAS ADAMS

CHAPTER 2

ANYTIME LUNCH

Avocado Toast 36

Chopped Greek Salad 41

Easy Egg Salad 42

Perfectly Hard-Boiled Eggs 44

Spring Pasta with Butter Sauce 46

Melty Pesto Paninis 49

Extra-Special Quesadillas 51

Hand-Pressed Tortillas 52

Taco Party 55

Taco Toppers: Curtido, Cucumber Salsa Fresca, and Sautéed Things 56

Sizzling Fried Rice 60

Summer Rolls with Peanut Sauce 64

AVOCADO TOAST

Creamy avocado toast never disappoints. It's the ultimate snacky-lunch—just cut, mash, and enjoy. Start with a fresh, ripe avocado and a really good-tasting loaf of bread to make the most of this simple dish. Avocados are heavenly all on their own; if you don't care for bread, halve the avocado, add oil, salt, and pepper, and eat it with a spoon.

you will need

Measuring spoons,
paring knife, spoon, fork

ingredients

1 ripe avocado (see Notes)

2 slices rustic or
country-style bread

Coarse salt

Ground black pepper

¼ teaspoon olive oil

preparation

1 Using a paring knife, cut the avocado in half and then remove the pit and peel the skin (see page 38).

2 Place one avocado half on a cutting board and cut the flesh into ¼-inch slices. Repeat with the second half and set both aside.

3 Toast the bread.

4 Layer the avocado slices onto the toast. Sprinkle with a **pinch** of salt and pepper, and gently mash with a fork. Drizzle the olive oil over the top.

NOTES

To tell if an avocado is ripe, do a little Goldilocks test. Gently pick it up with one hand. Is it rock-hard? Definitely unripe. Does the skin seem to collapse into the flesh? Definitely overripe. If the avocado gives way under your fingers, only slightly, it is *juuuust* right.

To ripen an avocado overnight, place it in a paper bag with a ripe banana. Bananas, avocados, and apples produce ethylene gas—a plant hormone that triggers ripening. Inside the bag, ethylene from the banana will be absorbed by the avocado and speed up the softening process.

If you like a little spice, try red pepper flakes on top!

HOW TO OPEN AN AVOCADO

1.
Set the avocado on a cutting surface and use a sharp knife to slice around the pit lengthwise.

2.
Turn the avocado over and cut lengthwise on the other side to cut the avocado in half.

3.
Twist both halves in opposite directions to separate.

4.
With the avocado lying on the cutting board, pierce the pit with the tip of the knife and twist gently to remove it. Peel the halves by hand and slice or cut according to the recipe.

CHOPPED GREEK SALAD

Greek salad, full of big, bright bites of fresh cucumbers and tomatoes, tastes like summer in a bowl. And yes, it does originate from Greece, where every seaside village has their own take on this national favorite. Maybe they like it for the same reason that I do—a bit of chopping and a crumble of salty feta cheese makes for a super-satisfying lunch or snack on the quick!

you will need

Measuring cups, measuring spoons, mixing bowl, chef's knife, small spoon, wooden spoon

ingredients

3 medium ripe tomatoes

½ cup fresh parsley leaves

3 small cucumbers

⅓ cup pitted Kalamata olives

3 ounces feta cheese, crumbled (about ½ cup)

2 tablespoons fresh lemon juice (from about 1 lemon)

Coarse salt

2 tablespoons olive oil

preparation

1 **Chop** the tomatoes into a large **dice**: slice them in half, then, with the flat side down, slice each half into thirds **lengthwise**, and then into thirds **crosswise**. (Remember to use "the claw" to protect your fingers.) Put into a mixing bowl. Chop the parsley leaves.

2 Peel the cucumbers, if you like, and cut off and discard the ends. Cut the cucumbers in half lengthwise and use a small spoon to scrape out the seeds. With the flat sides down, slice the cucumbers into half-moons, about ½ inch thick, then cut the half-moons into thirds. Add the cucumbers to the tomatoes.

3 Slice the olives into four pieces each and add them to the salad along with the feta cheese.

4 Pour the lemon juice over the salad, sprinkle with a **pinch** of salt, and stir with a wooden spoon so the salad is coated evenly with juice and the ingredients are mixed together. Add the olive oil and stir again. Taste and adjust the seasoning.

5 Heap the salad into serving bowls and sprinkle with a few pinches of chopped parsley. Eat right away.

EASY EGG SALAD

The best egg salad starts with a perfectly hard-boiled egg—in this case, one that has a creamy yolk inside. Add a **pinch** of salt and pepper, a dab of mustard and mayo, and lunch is served. Egg salad is a good bet for feeding a hungry crowd—as in your whole family, or maybe just your big brother. To make more, add 1 egg and 1 slice of toast per person.

you will need

Measuring spoons,
knife, small bowl, fork

ingredients

2 hard-boiled eggs
(see page 44)

Coarse salt

Ground black pepper

¼ teaspoon Dijon mustard

¼ teaspoon mayonnaise,
plus more for the bread

A few sprigs fresh dill or
parsley, minced (optional)

2 slices toast

preparation

1 Carefully slice the eggs in half and, with the cut side down, **chop** them into small pieces, about the size of sunflower seeds. (Remember to use "the claw" to protect your fingers.) Put the chopped eggs into a small bowl and mash them up just a little bit with the back of a fork.

2 Stir a pinch of salt and pepper (or more if you like) into the eggs, then mix in the mustard, mayonnaise, and dill (if using). Spread a thin layer of mayonnaise over the toast and layer the egg salad over that. Sprinkle with salt and pepper and enjoy!

PERFECTLY HARD-BOILED EGGS

Learn to boil an egg and you'll have a fast and fabulous breakfast, lunch, dinner, or snack at your fingertips for life. After that, whether you dress them up with olive oil and salt, turn them into egg salad, **chop** them into potato salad (or something else really clever and tasty) is all up to you.

you will need

Measuring spoons, measuring cup, medium saucepan, ladle, timer, medium bowl, paring knife

ingredients

2 eggs

5 or 6 ice cubes (for cooling the eggs)

Coarse salt

Ground black pepper

½ teaspoon olive oil (optional)

preparation

1 Put 4 cups water into a medium saucepan, place over high heat, and bring to a **boil**.

2 When the water reaches a boil, add the eggs, one at a time, using a ladle to set them gently into the water, so the shell doesn't crack. Set a timer for 8 minutes.

3 While the eggs are cooking, fill a medium bowl with the ice cubes and 2 cups cold water.

4 At 8 minutes, turn off the stove. Using the ladle, immediately remove the eggs from the boiling water and place them directly into the ice water for 2 minutes. This keeps them from overcooking. (If you don't plan to eat them right away, store in the refrigerator for up to 1 day.)

5 Once the eggs are cool, peel (see below) and, using a paring knife, slice them in half and dress with a **pinch** of salt and pepper and, if you like, a drizzle of olive oil (about ⅛ teaspoon per half).

6 Serve immediately.

HOW TO PEEL A HARD-BOILED EGG

Place the egg on a counter or a plate. Place your palm over the top, put a little pressure on the egg—just until you hear the first crunch of the shell—and then roll the egg back and forth underneath your palm, maintaining that slight pressure. When the shell has cracked in several places, pick up the egg and peel it by hand.

DID YOU KNOW?

* EGGS HAVE A SEASON, TOO! Chickens lay most of their eggs in the spring, just like so many other animals that deliver their young at that time.

* WHY DON'T THEY HATCH? The kind of eggs we eat can never hatch. They are unfertilized.

* WHY DO SOME EGGS HAVE A DEEP YELLOW, ALMOST ORANGE, YOLK? Pasture-raised, organic eggs are raised on healthful, green grass that lends a rich color to the yolk. It's a sign of good health for the chicken, and good nutrition for you!

* WHY ARE EGGSHELLS DIFFERENT COLORS? How many colors do they come in? Different chicken breeds lay different colored eggs. The most common colors are blue, brown, and white. Quail eggs, about one-fourth the size of a hen's egg, and very fun to eat, are speckled brown and white.

* HOW MANY WAYS ARE THERE TO COOK AN EGG? Scrambled, poached, fried, baked, hard-boiled, soft-boiled, custard-style, sunny-side up, over-easy, over-medium, over-well, omelette . . . to name just a few!

SPRING PASTA WITH BUTTER SAUCE

Here are three simple tips for outstanding pasta: #1—Use *lots* of salt in the cooking water. Some chefs call it a "4-finger **pinch**," roughly a heaping 1 teaspoon for 1 pound of pasta. #2—Dress the pasta with a drizzle of olive oil and stir it up right after you **drain** it. This keeps the noodles from sticking together. #3—Save some of the salty, starchy cooking water before you drain the pasta to thicken up your sauce, like we do here. *This last one is a great trick to have up your sleeve.*

you will need

Measuring cups, measuring spoons, stockpot, colander, knife, heatproof mixing bowl big enough to rest on the stockpot without falling in, oven mitt, ladle

Ingredients

Coarse salt

Few sprigs fresh parsley and marjoram or oregano

1 pound dried angel hair pasta or spaghettini

2 tablespoons unsalted butter

1 tablespoon olive oil

½ cup (heaping) grated Parmesan cheese

Ground black pepper

preparation

1 In a stockpot, combine 10 cups water and 2 tablespoons salt. Cover, place over high heat, and bring to a **boil**. Set a colander in the sink.

2 While the water is heating, pull the herb leaves from their stems (discard the stems) and **chop** the leaves fine (the size of ants; remember to use "the claw" to protect your fingers). You need 1 tablespoon of each chopped herb.

3 When the water is boiling, add the pasta and cook according to the package directions. Put the butter and olive oil into a heatproof mixing bowl and set it on top of the stockpot. When the butter is melted, use an oven mitt to move the bowl to the countertop. When the pasta is done cooking, turn off the stove.

4 Ladle ½ cup of the pasta cooking water into a measuring cup and then pour the pasta into the colander in the sink. Move the drained pasta to the mixing bowl with the butter and oil.

5 Add the herbs, cheese, and 1 tablespoon cooking water to the pasta and stir well. The "sauce" should be melty but not soupy— add another teaspoon or two of water to the sauce if needed. Taste a small bite and add salt or pepper as you like.

6 Serve warm, right from the mixing bowl.

TIPS

Store fresh herbs in a clean, damp dishcloth in the refrigerator to keep them fresh. First, run the cloth under cold water and then wring it out well. Lay the herbs in the cloth and roll up gently like a loose burrito. Herbs will keep this way for up to 3 days.

To see if pasta is cooked, scoop out a piece with a long-handled spoon or fork. Let it cool a moment and then bite into it. It should be tender, with a little firmness, but no crunch.

MELTY PESTO PANINIS

This recipe is a double header—you'll end up with a top-notch sandwich *and* you'll learn to make pesto, with enough left over from lunch to dress a pound of pasta for dinner. In the summer, add fresh tomato slices and make it a *caprese*— a traditional Italian salad (and now sandwich) of mozzarella, tomato, and basil.

you will need

Measuring cups, measuring spoons, knife, food processor, rubber spatula, small bowl, small sauté pan, aluminum foil, paper towels, small skillet, spatula

ingredients

FOR THE PESTO

2 garlic cloves

2 bunches basil (about 1½ cups leaves, lightly **packed**)

½ cup chopped fresh parsley

½ cup olive oil

½ teaspoon coarse salt

¼ cup grated Parmesan cheese

FOR THE SANDWICHES

8 slices fresh mozzarella cheese

1 sprig basil

1 to 2 teaspoons pesto

4 thick slices bread

1½ teaspoons olive oil

Coarse salt

Ground black pepper

preparation

Make the pesto

1 Peel and **chop** the garlic. (Remember to use "the claw" to protect your fingers.) Pull the basil leaves from their stems (discard the stems).

2 In a food processor, combine the garlic, basil, parsley, olive oil, and salt. Turn on the processor and count to 20. Use a rubber spatula to scrape down the sides of the processor and then replace the lid and pulse again, for another count of 20. Repeat until the ingredients are blended into a paste. The pesto won't be completely smooth; it will still have pieces of herbs roughly the size of ants, but the garlic should be completely mashed.

3 Transfer the pesto to a small bowl and stir in the Parmesan cheese. The pesto will keep in a tightly sealed container in the freezer for up to 1 month.

Make the sandwiches

1 Cover the outside bottom of a small sauté pan with aluminum foil so that the foil wraps up the sides and over the lip of the pan. Then, line a cutting board with two paper towels.

2 Arrange the mozzarella cheese slices on the prepared cutting board and pat them dry with another paper towel.

3 Pull the leaves from the basil sprig and then **chiffonade** (roll into a pencil shape and slice thinly them).

CONTINUED

4 Spread the pesto (add more if you are a big fan!) over two of the bread slices. Spoon 1/4 teaspoon of the olive oil over each of the other two slices. Arrange the cheese on top of the pesto, drizzle with the remaining 1 teaspoon olive oil, and add a **pinch** of salt and pepper and a sprinkle of chiffonaded basil. Close the sandwiches.

5 In a small skillet over medium heat, toast the sandwiches for about 2 minutes. While the sandwiches are cooking, take the foil-covered pan by the handle and press the bottom down firmly onto the sandwiches to flatten them. Flip the sandwiches over with a spatula and flatten the other sides. Cook until the bread is toasty and the cheese begins to melt.

6 Move the sandwiches to plates and eat them while they're warm and melty.

TASTE WITH YOUR NOSE

Smell impacts tastes more than you might think. From our taste buds, we really get only basic sensations of sweet, sour, bitter, salty, and savory (the rich, round flavor of things like butter). While you eat, odor molecules escape from the food and rise up with your breath to your nose. On the way, they hit your brain's "smell" messengers that allow you to experience complex flavors. This explains why it's hard to "taste" food when you have a stuffed-up nose!

EXTRA-SPECIAL QUESADILLAS

These quesadillas are even tastier than the usual kind because they're stuffed with cheese *and* fluffy scrambled eggs. When I was growing up, family vacations were all about the quesadilla brunch. My dad would sneak out first thing in the morning while we slept snug in our bunks and come back to fry up fresh-caught fish alongside his famous quesadillas. Now we eat them (without the fish!) for a warm and melty lunch or brunch a couple of times a week.

you will need

Measuring spoons, grater, 2 small bowls, knife, small spoon, whisk, small sauté pan (preferably nonstick), rubber spatula, griddle, spatula

ingredients

2 to 3 ounces Cheddar or Monterey Jack cheese

A few sprigs fresh cilantro

4 eggs

1 tablespoon plain, whole-milk yogurt (not Greek style)

Coarse salt

Ground black pepper

1½ teaspoons olive oil

2 Hand-Pressed Tortillas (page 52) or store-bought

Hot sauce or salsa for serving (optional)

preparation

1   Grate the cheese into a small bowl. Pull the cilantro leaves from the stems and **chop** them (a little stem is okay; remember to use "the claw" to protect your fingers).

2   In another small bowl, crack the eggs, removing any shell with a spoon. Whisk in the yogurt and a **pinch** of salt and pepper until the eggs and yogurt are completely combined.

3   Put 1 teaspoon of the olive oil in a small sauté pan, use a rubber spatula to coat the bottom of the pan, and place over medium heat for about 1 minute. To test the heat, drop a bead of water into the pan. If it sizzles and evaporates (disappears) immediately, the pan is ready. Pour in the eggs all at once, and turn the heat to low. Stir constantly, gently scraping the bottom of the pan and folding the eggs over on themselves for about 2 minutes. When eggs are just **set** (firm), sprinkle with a pinch of salt and pepper.

4   On a clean griddle, drizzle the remaining ½ teaspoon olive oil and turn the heat to medium-high. Count to 20. Using the spatula, lay the tortillas flat on the griddle and heat until they start to soften, about 1 minute. Flip them over with the spatula and then sprinkle the grated cheese over the top. When the cheese is melty, move the tortillas to a plate and then turn off the stove.

5   Heap the eggs onto one side of each tortilla. Fold the tortillas in half, pressing down gently to close, and top with the chopped cilantro and salsa, if you like. Serve warm.

HAND-PRESSED TORTILLAS

These cakey tortillas are fun to make and so much better than the store-bought kind. And, you can make tortillas in less time than it would take you to go to the store to buy them. Don't believe it? Take this challenge: Time yourself making this recipe, and then time yourself going to the store and back with your packaged tortillas. I think you'll like these homemade ones better, too.

you will need

Measuring cups, measuring spoons, large bowl, whisk, wooden spoon, clean kitchen towel, parchment paper, small sauté pan, heavy-bottomed skillet

ingredients

1 cup masa harina (see Note)

1 teaspoon coarse salt

¾ cup cold water

preparation

1 In a large bowl, whisk together the masa harina and salt. Slowly add the water and mix gently with a wooden spoon until all the liquid is absorbed and a dough forms. Cover the dough with a clean kitchen towel and set it aside for 10 minutes.

2 After resting, the dough should be soft and smooth, not crumbly or sticky. (If it crumbles, add a drop of water; if it sticks to your hands, add a **pinch** of masa harina. Then, **knead** the ingredients together.) Divide the dough evenly into eight pieces (or four pieces for large tortillas) and roll each piece into a ball.

3 Place one ball on a large piece of parchment paper—about the size of a sheet of paper—to the right of center. Fold the paper over onto the ball and press down very lightly with the bottom of a small sauté pan or the palm of your hand to flatten it into a thin round, no thicker than a piece of cardboard. Peel the paper away from both sides of the tortilla at once. (If it sticks, re-roll slightly thicker or **dust** the parchment with a pinch of masa harina and try again.) Repeat with the rest of the dough.

4 Warm a heavy-bottomed skillet over medium-high heat (or an electric griddle to 350°F). To test the heat, drop a bead of water into the pan. If it sizzles and evaporates (disappears) immediately, the pan is ready. Add the tortillas and cook until golden brown spots appear, about 3 minutes per side. Stack the finished tortillas on a plate and cover with a clean kitchen towel. When all the tortillas are finished cooking, turn off the stove, and serve them warm.

NOTE

Masa harina is available at most supermarkets or Mexican grocery stores and online. For the best tortillas, choose standard masa harina rather than any type that is labeled "instant."

TACO PARTY

These "build-your-own" tacos are as much fun to serve as they are to eat. With so many fillings to choose from, everyone gets to invent their own idea of taco heaven. When it's time to eat, we fill the table with all the different toppings laid out in colorful bowls, and have ourselves a taco party. This recipe makes a base taco of cheese, beans, and avocado. Choose one or more toppers to amp up your meal.

you will need

Measuring cups, measuring spoons, knife, grater, small bowl, medium-mesh strainer, small saucepan, griddle, spatula, wooden spoon

ingredients

1 lime

1 ripe avocado (see Note, page 36)

3 ounces Cheddar or Monterey Jack cheese

2 cups cooked black beans (one 15-ounce can)

¼ teaspoon ground cumin

¼ teaspoon ground chile powder (optional)

1 tablespoon olive oil, plus 1 teaspoon

¼ teaspoon salt (if the beans are "no salt added")

½ bunch fresh cilantro

Taco Toppers
(see pages 56 to 58)

Six 6-inch tortillas
(see page 52)

Hot sauce for serving

preparation

1 On a cutting board, quarter the lime. Slice the avocado (see page 38) and place on a small plate; squeeze one lime quarter over the top. Grate the cheese into a small bowl and set that aside with the remaining lime wedges and avocado. **Drain** and rinse the beans in a medium-mesh strainer.

2 In a small saucepan, combine the beans, cumin, chile powder, 1 tablespoon olive oil, and salt (if using). Place over medium-low heat and warm for 10 minutes. Stir, taste, and adjust the seasonings as you like.

3 Rinse the cilantro and shake it dry. **Chop** the cilantro leaves once or twice; whole leaves and a little stem are fine—even a good addition. (Remember to use "the claw" to protect your fingers.) Add the chopped cilantro to the plate of avocado and lime. Set on the table along with the beans and toppers.

4 Coat a griddle with the remaining 1 teaspoon olive oil (spread it around with the edge of a spatula) and warm over medium-low heat for 1 minute. Put the tortillas onto the griddle; all six at once if they can fit. Warm the tortillas for 1 minute, then flip them over with the spatula and add a heaping spoonful of grated cheese to each one. Turn off the stove.

5 Put two warm tortillas on each plate. Layer on beans and whatever other toppings you like.

6 Douse the tacos with hot sauce, pick up, fold over, and close your eyes to get the full effect of that first, mouthwatering bite.

TACO TOPPERS

If you're making all the toppings (excellent choice!), make the curtido first, then the salsa, followed by the sautéed things—then the basic tacos—in that order.

CURTIDO

Makes enough to top 6 tacos

you will need

Measuring spoons, vegetable peeler, medium bowl, box grater, small spoon, knife, mixing spoon

ingredients

1 large carrot

¼ head green or purple cabbage

1 small jicama

1 jalapeño chile (optional)

1 lime

1½ teaspoons apple cider vinegar

Coarse salt

2 tablespoons chopped fresh cilantro

preparation

1   Peel and trim the carrot, then shave it into long ribbons using a vegetable peeler. When the carrot gets too small to peel wide ribbons, stop peeling and snack on the rest. Put the ribbons in a medium bowl.

2   Using the large holes of a box grater, grate the cabbage into the carrot bowl.

3   Slice the jicama in half. With the cut side down, peel it with the peeler. Work from the top to trim away the skin (discard it). Grate half of the jicama on the medium holes of the grater and add to the cabbage and carrot.

4   If you're using a jalapeño, cut it in half **lengthwise**. Use a small spoon to scoop out the white core and seeds and discard them. Turn one half over so the cut side is facedown and slice it into thin half-moons, about ⅛ inch thick. **Chop** the half-moons into small pieces and add them to the cabbage. (Remember to use "the claw" to protect your fingers.)

5   Cut the lime into quarters. Squeeze three wedges over the cabbage, and **reserve** one to squeeze over your tacos.

6   Using a mixing spoon, stir the vinegar and a **pinch** of salt into the bowl. *Let the salad sit for 15 minutes.* Sprinkle with the cilantro just before serving.

CUCUMBER SALSA FRESCA

Makes about 2 cups

you will need

Measuring spoons, knife, small spoon, small bowl

ingredients

1 medium cucumber

2 medium ripe tomatoes

1 jalapeño chile (optional)

1 garlic clove

1 tablespoon fresh lime juice (from about ½ lime)

1 teaspoon white vinegar (optional)

Coarse salt

1 tablespoon (heaping) chopped fresh cilantro

preparation

1. On a cutting board, trim the ends from the cucumber, peel it, and slice it in half **lengthwise**. Use a small spoon to scrape out the seeds. Set one half cut-side down and slice it lengthwise down the middle, then **crosswise** into ¼-inch pieces (about the size of a thumbtack) to cut it into a small **dice**. Put the cucumber in a small bowl.

2. Slice the **stem end** from the tomatoes, then cut the tomatoes in half starting where the stem used to be. With the cut sides down, make ¼-inch slices lengthwise, then make ¼-inch slices crosswise for a small dice (about the same size as the cucumbers). Add these to the cucumbers.

3. If you're using the jalapeño, cut four or five paper-thin slices from the bottom half (not the stem end), chop into ant-size pieces, and add them to the other vegetables. Wash your hands and cutting surface with warm water and soap before moving on to the next step.

4. Peel the garlic, cut it in half, and drop it into the bowl. Add the lime juice, vinegar (if using), and a **pinch** of salt. Stir once or twice, let the salsa sit at room temperature for about 10 minutes, and then stir in the chopped cilantro.

5. Remove the garlic just before serving.

HEADS UP

The oil from chiles, especially their seeds, can burn! Don't touch your eyes or body when working with chiles. Be sure to wash the cutting board and your hands with hot water and soap afterward.

SAUTÉED THINGS

Makes enough to top 6 tacos

you will need

Measuring spoons, paring knife, cast-iron or nonstick skillet, wooden spoon

ingredients

1 bunch green onions

1 medium zucchini

1 tablespoon olive oil

¼ teaspoon coarse salt

preparation

1. Using a paring knife, trim as little as possible from the root ends of the green onions (the part with the "hairs") and most of the top, leaving about 3 inches of the white and light green part.

2. Trim the ends of the zucchini and cut it in half **crosswise**. Stand one half on a cutting board. Cut into three even slices. Lay the slices down and cut into ¼-inch strips, about the size of a skinny french fry. Repeat with the second half of the zucchini.

3. In a cast-iron or nonstick skillet over high heat, warm the olive oil. Count to 30 and then check the oil. If it has started to move around in the pan, it's ready. Add the green onions, zucchini, and salt; turn the heat to medium-high; and stir with a wooden spoon for 3 to 4 minutes, until the vegetables are soft and nicely browned on the edges. Turn off the stove.

Transfer the vegetables to a plate and serve warm.

Cucumber Salsa Fresca

Curtido

Sautéed Things

SIZZLING FRIED RICE

Fried rice is a grand way to use up leftover rice (and, really, what else are you going to do with it?). Once you have the hang of it, you can whip up a fancy-ish meal on the fly with pretty much whatever you find in the fridge. Give the vegetables a quick **sauté** with a few spices for good measure, toss them with the rice, and ta-da! Your meal is ready—scrumptious, warm, and so much better because it was prepared by you.

you will need

Measuring cups, measuring spoons, grater, knife, vegetable peeler, large sauté pan, wooden spoon, medium bowl

ingredients

2½-inch piece fresh ginger

2 small garlic cloves

3 to 4 ounces snap peas (about 2 handfuls) or 1 head baby bok choy

1 large carrot

2 tablespoons sesame oil

Coarse salt

4 tablespoons water

2 cups cooked jasmine, basmati, or brown rice (see "How to Cook Rice," page 63)

2 teaspoons soy sauce

2 teaspoons toasted black or brown sesame seeds (optional)

preparation

1 Peel and grate the ginger and peel and **mince** the garlic (see page 8). Remove the "string" from the snap peas by pinching the stem with your fingers and pulling it down along the length of the pod. Repeat on the other end to remove the string from the other side. Cut each snap pea into three pieces **on the bias** (diagonally).

2 Peel the carrot and trim the ends. Lay it on a cutting board and cut it in half **lengthwise**. With the cut side down, and using the tip of the paring knife, cut each half into three long strips. Rotate the pieces and cut them **crosswise** into a medium **dice** (about the size of a thumbtack).

3 In a large sauté pan over medium-high heat, warm 1 tablespoon of the sesame oil. Count to 20, add the garlic and ginger, stir three or four times with a wooden spoon, and then add the carrot.

4 Stir ¼ teaspoon salt and 2 tablespoons of the water into the pan and cook, stirring, until the carrot begins to soften, about 2 minutes. Add the peas, a **pinch** of salt, and the remaining 2 tablespoons water and cook, stirring, until the vegetables begin to soften and brown at the edges, another 2 to 3 minutes. Scoop all the vegetables into a medium bowl and then turn the heat to low.

CONTINUED

VARIATION

Replace the vegetables with 2½ cups of cabbage or green beans (or a combination) and stir in scrambled eggs at the very end.

DID YOU KNOW?

In one year alone, we threw away enough food in this country to fill the Empire State Building *91 times*! Using up leftover rice is a small step toward reducing that waste. Other ways you can make a difference are to **compost** or freeze your leftovers, take smaller portions, and plan your meals.

5 Add the remaining 1 tablespoon sesame oil to the pan. Count to 30, then spread the rice out across the pan and turn the heat to high.

6 Cook the rice until it sizzles, about 10 seconds, then stir and flatten it back down until you hear it sizzle again. Do this a few times to fry all of the rice, stirring quickly so it doesn't burn. If the rice begins to burn, turn the heat to medium. Stir in the vegetables and soy sauce and then turn off the stove.

7 Serve warm, sprinkled with the sesame seeds.

HOW TO COOK RICE

Use the amounts of rice and water suggested on the package, usually about 2 cups water to 1 cup rice. Always rinse rice before cooking. Put it in a bowl, cover it with water, and swish with your fingers to remove any debris. **Drain** the rice in a fine-mesh strainer. Put the rinsed rice in a medium saucepan with fresh water and about ¼ teaspoon salt. Bring it to a rolling **boil** over high heat. When the water reaches a boil, turn the heat to low. Cover the rice and let it cook 20 minutes for white rice, 50 minutes for brown rice, or until it is tender but not sticky (overcooked). If the rice is still crunchy, turn off the stove, replace the lid, and allow it to sit for another 10 to 20 minutes.

SUMMER ROLLS WITH PEANUT SAUCE

Summer rolls (fresh) and spring rolls (fried) are the ultimate fast food—a portable meal in an edible container! The wrappers seem like magic, too. They start out dry and brittle, but with a little dip in water they become soft and translucent. The real trick is in the rolling. Take it slow, and your patience will be rewarded.

you will need

Measuring cups, measuring spoons, small spoon or vegetable peeler, blender, small bowl, small plate, chef's knife, large bowl, paring knife, zester, medium bowl

ingredients

FOR THE PEANUT SAUCE

1-inch piece fresh ginger

2 tablespoons soy sauce

2 tablespoons fresh lime juice (from about 1½ limes)

1 small garlic clove

½ cup smooth peanut butter (no sugar added)

½ cup water

2 teaspoons brown sugar

¼ teaspoon red pepper flakes

preparation

Make the peanut sauce

1 Peel the ginger by scraping it with the side of a small spoon or a vegetable peeler.

2 In a blender, combine the ginger, soy sauce, lime juice, and garlic. **Blend**, starting on low speed and gradually working up to medium-high speed, until a smooth paste forms, 1 minute or less.

3 Add the peanut butter, water, brown sugar, and red pepper flakes. Blend on medium-high speed until smooth and about the same consistency as pancake batter—not runny, but not sticky. Add more water, 1 tablespoon at a time, if the sauce is too thick to pour. Transfer to a small bowl.

CONTINUED

NOTE

Summer rolls are great with all kinds of produce! If you don't have the ingredients listed, try them with things you do have on hand, like lettuce, tofu, or red bell pepper.

FOR THE ROLLS

1 ripe avocado
(see Note, page 36)

½ bunch basil

½ bunch cilantro

½ bunch mint

2 medium cucumbers

4 medium carrots

1 lime

1 tablespoon olive oil

1 tablespoon sesame oil

½ teaspoon rice vinegar

Coarse salt

Ten 6-inch round rice paper wrappers (available at most supermarkets in the "international" aisle)

Make the rolls

1 Cut the avocado into ¼-inch slices (see page 38) and scoop them out onto a small plate. Pull the basil, cilantro, and mint leaves from the stems (discard the stems) and, using a chef's knife, **chop** the leaves into smaller pieces, about pea-size. (Remember to use "the claw" to protect your fingers.) Transfer to a large bowl.

2 Trim and discard the ends of the cucumbers and carrots. Peel them with a vegetable peeler and discard the outer peel. Continue peeling the vegetables into long thin ribbons. Then, lay the ribbons flat on a cutting board and cut them in half **crosswise**. Stack the pieces on top of one another and cut them **lengthwise** into matchstick-size pieces. Add these to the herbs.

3 Using a zester, **zest** half of the lime into the vegetables, then juice the lime. Add 2 teaspoons lime juice, the olive oil, sesame oil, rice vinegar, and a **pinch** of salt to the vegetables. Mix well.

4 Fill a medium bowl with warm water. Dip a rice paper wrapper into the water and swish for 5 seconds. When the wrapper is wet but not soaking, shake off the excess water and lay the wrapper flat on the cutting board.

5 Put ¼ cup of the vegetable mixture onto half of the wrapper and top with a slice of avocado. (The skin may break if the roll is too full.) Fold the sides of the wrapper in toward the middle, hold the sides in, and roll the wrapper from the bottom up toward the top until you have what looks like a very thin burrito. Repeat with the remaining wrappers and vegetable mixture.

6 Serve the rolls with the peanut sauce, and dip to your heart's content.

 TIP

This recipe calls for lime zest, which comes from the outer skin, so it's extra important to choose limes that have not been sprayed with pesticides.

HOW TO ROLL A SUMMER ROLL

1.
Place filling onto lower half of wrapper.

2.
Fold sides of wrapper in.

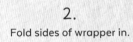

3.
Holding sides, roll wrapper up from the bottom. If it doesn't stick together, dab a little water along the edge to seal it closed.

> What could be more important than a little something to eat?
>
> —WINNIE-THE-POOH

CHAPTER 3

IN-BETWEEN MEALS AND AFTER-SCHOOL SNACKS

Peanut Butter Power Shake 70

Melon Wedges with Lime 73

Zesty Mango and Cucumber 74

Thick and Creamy Homemade Hummus 79

Three-Minute Guacamole with Fresh Chips 80

Fire-Roasted Corn On (or Off) the Cob 83

Crispy Cauliflower Poppers 87

Sweet Potato Fries 88

Pan-Fried Flatbreads with Spiced Butter 91

PEANUT BUTTER POWER SHAKE

Chocolate, peanut butter, banana? Yes! The only question is, frozen or fresh? It's true that frozen bananas give shakes a more ice-creamy texture. But in the freezer, bananas and other fruit can lose a lot of flavor and even pick up some funky aromas. So I always vote for fresh when available, and use ice cubes to make it cool and creamy. If you're a frozen-banana fan, use only three ice cubes and adjust the amount of milk to make the shake as thick as you like.

you will need

Measuring cup, measuring spoons, blender

ingredients

2 small, ripe (but not squishy!) bananas

1½ cups milk or almond milk (see Note)

1 tablespoon plus 1 teaspoon creamy, unsweetened peanut butter

1 tablespoon plus 1 teaspoon honey

2 teaspoons unsweetened cocoa powder

A **pinch** of coarse salt

10 ice cubes

preparation

1 Peel the bananas and break them in two.

2 In a blender, combine the bananas, milk, peanut butter, honey, cocoa powder, and salt, then add the ice cubes. Make sure the top of the blender is on and tightly fastened. **Blend**, starting on low speed and gradually working up to the highest setting. Count to 20, turn off the blender, and use a spoon to check the consistency.

3 The shake should be thick and smooth, with no pieces of ice rattling around and no streaks of peanut butter. If needed, close the lid tightly and blend again for another 20 to 30 seconds.

4 Pour into tall glasses and drink immediately.

NOTE

If you prefer a thicker
shake, start with 1 cup milk
and add more if needed.

TIP

To store a half melon, simply place it cut-side down on a plate in the refrigerator. If any flesh is exposed, cover the plate tightly with plastic wrap.

MELON WEDGES WITH LIME

When summer is in full tilt, the best afternoon snack is one that doubles as a refreshing drink, too. This sweet and juicy combo does the trick. A squeeze of lime juice works wonders for melon that's not quite at its peak, drawing out even more flavor from summer's sweetest crop. Feel free to substitute any melon that is available and in season.

you will need

Chef's knife

ingredients

1 lime

½ ripe honeydew melon

½ ripe cantaloupe melon

preparation

1 On a cutting board, quarter the lime.

2 Place each melon cut-side down on a cutting board. Using a chef's knife, slice the melons into quarters. Put each quarter skin-side down on the cutting board and remove the rind by placing the knife at the tip closest to you and cutting underneath the flesh from one tip of the slice to the other, with the knife moving away from you.

3 Cut the melon quarters in half and arrange on a small plate. Squeeze half the lime over the melon (or **to taste**).

4 Eat immediately.

HOW DO I TELL IF A MELON IS RIPE?

Smell the **blossom end** (the belly button opposite the **stem end**). It should smell sweet and fragrant. If not, it may need a few days to ripen at room temperature.

ZESTY MANGO AND CUCUMBER

In tropical (hot-weather) countries, the food tends to be spicy—supposedly because heating yourself up from the inside is a good way to cool down on the outside. That's how it works with this little bit of mango heaven. Hot weather or not, you won't want to stop until you've licked the plate clean.

you will need

Measuring spoons, paring knife, medium bowl, small bowl

ingredients

1 lime

1 ripe mango (see Note)

1 medium cucumber

¼ teaspoon ground ancho chile powder

Coarse salt

preparation

1   On a cutting board, quarter the lime.

2   Peel and slice the mango (see "How to Cut a Mango," page 76). Cut the slices into ½-inch-wide spears and place in a medium bowl.

3   Peel the cucumbers, discard the ends, and slice them in half, **crosswise**. Slice each half down the center, **lengthwise**. Place the cut side down on the cutting board and slice each piece into spears. Add the spears to the mango slices and stir to combine.

4   In a small bowl, combine the chile powder and a **pinch** or two of salt. Taste a tiny bit and add a pinch more salt if you like.

5   Squeeze a wedge of lime over the fruit and sprinkle with a pinch or two of the chile powder mixture. Taste the fruit and add more lime juice or seasoning, as you like.

6   Devour immediately!

DID YOU KNOW?

Cucumber peel is perfectly edible. Depending on the variety of cucumber, some skin can be thick and bitter while others are thin and sweet. English, Japanese, and Persian cucumbers generally have tastier skin that will add a nice crunch and color to your dish. If you're leaving the skin on, wash the cucumber well before preparing.

NOTE

To tell if a mango is ripe, pick it up and gently squeeze it—it should feel soft but not squishy. A ripe mango will have a fragrant aroma, and some varieties will ooze a clear "sap" from the **stem end**. The Ataulfo variety does not smell fragrant—instead the skin will be very slightly wrinkled when it's ready to eat.

HOW TO CUT A MANGO

A mango has an oblong flat pit in the middle that you have to cut around to get at the fruit.

1.
Stand the mango on one end. With the stem end up, slice off the sides, on either side of the stem, so you have three pieces.

2.
Hold one mango piece on a cutting board, peel-side down. For spears, cut lengthwise through the fruit but not the peel.

3.
For cubes, cut both lengthwise and crosswise

4.
Pull the skin back to separate the slices.

5.
Use a spoon to scoop the slices or cubes away from the peel.

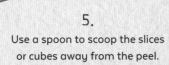

DID YOU KNOW?

Chickpeas, also known as garbanzo beans or ceci beans, are not actually a bean but a legume—a relative of peas—which is a seed contained inside a pod. Legumes are high in protein (great for vegetarians) and they are also *really good* for the soil, where they "fix" nitrogen—an important nutrient for plants—into a form the plants can readily use.

THICK AND CREAMY HOMEMADE HUMMUS

Hummus—a creamy spread of chickpeas and spices—is one of those things I love to eat and never knew I could just whip up right at home. In the Middle East, where hummus comes from, it is *everywhere all the time*! People eat it with breakfast, lunch, and dinner, and as a snack, along with toasty pita bread, crunchy pickles, and sliced fresh vegetables to dip. Hummus will keep in a tightly sealed container, refrigerated, for up to 5 days.

you will need

Measuring cups, measuring spoons, medium-mesh strainer, medium bowl, paring knife, blender or food processor, long-handled spoon

ingredients

One 15-ounce can chickpeas

2 lemons

1 small garlic clove

¼ cup tahini (see Note)

3 tablespoons olive oil

Coarse salt

A **pinch** of paprika

1 tablespoon chopped fresh flat-leaf parsley

Pita bread, carrots, cucumbers, and snap peas for dipping

preparation

1 In a strainer set over a medium bowl, **strain** the chickpeas and **reserve** the liquid. Juice the lemons and set the juice aside. Peel the garlic clove and, using a paring knife, slice it in half.

2 In a blender or food processor, combine the chickpeas, ¼ cup of the reserved liquid, ¼ cup lemon juice, the tahini, 1 tablespoon of the olive oil, 1 teaspoon salt, and half of the garlic. (If you are a garlic lover, use the whole clove.)

3 **Blend**, starting on low speed and gradually working up to the highest setting. Count to 20, then turn off the blender and remove the top. Using a long-handled spoon, check the consistency; if the texture is dry, add another 2 tablespoons reserved chickpea liquid. Turn the blender back on and blend until the hummus is very smooth, about 30 seconds.

4 Taste a little bit and add salt or lemon juice in small amounts, if you like. Spoon the hummus into a shallow bowl, drizzle with the remaining 2 tablespoons olive oil, and sprinkle with the paprika, chopped parsley, and a bit of lemon juice. Serve immediately with pita bread and vegetables.

 NOTE

Tahini is a sesame spread, available in most grocery stores.

THREE-MINUTE GUACAMOLE WITH FRESH CHIPS

If you can get your hands on a good ripe avocado, you've got this snack nailed down. With a bag of store-bought chips, you'll be munching chips and guac in 3 minutes flat, but if you're looking for extra oomph, try your hand at this homemade chip recipe, too. Freshly made tortilla chips are crispy, crunchy, and way easier to make than you think!

You'll need an adult to help with this recipe because of the hot oil, which can bubble and pop up out of the pan and cause *serious burns*. When you're frying food, pay close attention, don't have any other burners going at the same time, turn on the oven fan, and use a long-handled tool to keep your arms and hands away from the hot oil.

you will need

Measuring cup, knife, small bowl, fork, large plate, paper towels, 9-inch cast-iron or other skillet at least 2 inches deep (see Note), cooking thermometer or clean wooden spoon, large bowl

ingredients

FOR THE GUACAMOLE

1 fresh chive stalk

1 lime

2 ripe avocados (see Note, page 36)

Coarse salt

preparation

Make the guacamole

1 **Mince** the chive stalk to the size of ants or smaller. Cut the lime into quarters. Slice the avocados (see page 38) and put them into a small bowl.

2 Sprinkle the avocados with a generous **pinch** of salt and the chives and add a squeeze of lime juice. Mash gently with the back of a fork to whatever consistency you prefer, making sure to mix in all the ingredients. Taste a bit and add lime juice or salt until it tastes right to you.

CONTINUED

This would also be so yummy on top of tacos!

FOR THE TORTILLA CHIPS

10 small tortillas (thinnest you can find; see page 52 to make your own!)

3 cups peanut or canola oil

Coarse salt

Make the chips

1 Line a large plate with four paper towels stacked one on top of the other.

2 Stack the tortillas in two sets of five and cut them into quarters.

3 In a 9-inch cast-iron skillet over medium-high heat, warm the peanut oil. Test the heat with a thermometer, it should be 350°F. If you don't have a thermometer, use the clean handle of a wooden spoon by touching it to the bottom of the pan; if bubbles rise up steadily from the wood, the oil is ready. If the bubbles are coming fast and furiously, turn down the heat a touch and count to 10 before adding the tortillas.

4 When the oil is ready, add the tortillas, five to eight wedges at a time, using a long-handled slotted spoon; don't crowd them. The oil will start to bubble around the chips. Use the slotted spoon to flip each one over several times until the oil stops bubbling and the chips begin to brown, about 2 minutes.

5 Use the slotted spoon to transfer chips to the prepared plate. Sprinkle with a generous pinch of salt, and let them cool a moment before moving them to a clean large bowl. Repeat the whole process with the rest of the tortilla wedges in another three batches. Change the paper towels when they start to get soaked, and check the temperature of the oil again with each batch. When the chips are done frying, turn off the stove.

6 Bring the bowl of chips and the bowl of guacamole to the table and dig in! These chips taste best when eaten right away, while they are still warm.

 NOTE

The size of the pan is important—if you're using a 12-inch skillet, you'll need an additional cup of oil for frying.

FIRE-ROASTED CORN ON (OR OFF) THE COB

The words *lip-smacking good* definitely describe this outrageously delicious corn. If you can stop eating halfway through, lick your lips clean—the salty, spicy, tangy coating is almost as good as the corn itself. If you don't have a stove-top grill or barbecue, just cut the kernels off the cob and **sauté** them on the stove.

you will need

Measuring spoons, paring knife, small bowl, stove-top grill or BBQ (for corn on the cob), tongs, wide shallow bowl, small sauté pan

ingredients

1 lime

¼ teaspoon paprika

¼ teaspoon coarse salt

A **pinch** of cayenne pepper (optional)

2 ears corn, still in the husk

1 teaspoon butter (for corn off the cob)

preparation

1 On a cutting board, cut the lime in half. In a small bowl, combine the paprika, salt, and cayenne and stir to mix.

On the Cob

1 Prepare a stove-top grill to cook over high heat or a BBQ to medium-high heat (with the help of an adult).

2 Put the corn (still in the husks) on the grill and cook for 5 minutes. Using a pair of tongs, turn them over once and cook for another 5 minutes. The husks should be blackened in a few spots. If not, cook the corn for another few minutes. Use the tongs to remove the corn from the grill. Turn off the stove.

3 When the corn is cool enough to handle, remove the husks and silky threads. Dip a lime half into the mixed spice and spread on one of the cobs. Dip the lime again if needed and rotate the ear of corn to get a good coating of spice over the whole thing. Use the other lime half on the second piece.

Off the Cob

1 Shuck the corn and pull off the silky threads. Snap or cut the cob in half and stand the half cob cut-side down in a wide shallow bowl (to catch the kernels). Using the paring knife, slice off the kernels, starting at the top of the cob and working straight downward.

CONTINUED

Work close to the cob but not so close that you feel friction—this means you're also cutting off the (unwanted) fibrous pieces where the kernel connects to the cob.

2 In a small sauté pan over medium-high heat, melt the butter. When it starts to bubble, add the kernels and turn the heat to high.

3 Cook until the kernels begin to brown, stirring the whole time, about 1 minute. If the kernels start to pop, turn the heat to medium-high.

4 Transfer the corn back to the bowl and turn off the stove. Add a squeeze of lime juice and two or three pinches of the mixed spice to the corn and stir. Taste and add more spice if needed.

5 Serve warm!

THE LEGEND OF THE THREE SISTERS

Corn is one of the "Three Sisters"—a legend told by Native Americans to pass on their way of "companion" planting. The story goes that the three sisters—corn, squash, and beans—were always together. In the field, corn grows a tall stalk, so it's planted first. Next come the beans, which use the stalk to hold up their ropy, climbing vines. The squash grows close to the ground, spreading its lush leaves over the soil to keep the water in, so the plants always have enough to drink. Each plant does their part to help the others grow. This clever way of planting is so effective, it is still used to this day.

CRISPY CAULIFLOWER POPPERS

You will never believe how good roasted cauliflower is until you try it for yourself. Roasting transforms those frumpy little **florets** into crispy, salty flavor bombs. At our house, we inhale cauliflower poppers while we're waiting for the rest of dinner to cook, so I always plan for a second batch to go with the meal.

you will need

Measuring spoons, chef's knife, large bowl, baking sheet

ingredients

1 head cauliflower

2 tablespoons olive oil

1 teaspoon coarse salt

A **pinch** or two of red pepper flakes (optional)

preparation

1 Preheat the oven to 475°F.

2 Using a knife, trim the stem and leaves from the bottom of the cauliflower. Turn the cauliflower stem-side down so it's resting flat on a cutting board. Slice through the cauliflower as if it's a loaf of bread, cutting ½-inch-thick slices. Break the florets away from the stem with your hands, or with the tip of your knife, making bite-size or slightly larger pieces.

3 Put the pieces in a large bowl, add the olive oil, and stir to coat them.

4 Arrange the pieces, with plenty of space between them, on a baking sheet and sprinkle with the salt.

5 **Bake** until the cauliflower gets nice and brown on top, 25 to 30 minutes. It may look like it's burning a bit at the edges but that's okay. Turn off the oven, remove the baking sheet, and allow the poppers to cool for 5 minutes.

6 Serve warm, and **garnish** with the red pepper flakes, if desired.

SWEET POTATO FRIES

This is my daughter Romy's after-school snack of choice. Roasty and soft, and just a little crispy on the outside, these baked sweet-potato "fries" are a cinch. Aside from peeling and slicing the potato, there's really nothing to it. Sweet potatoes go by many names; for this recipe, choose the ones with reddish skin and orange flesh, commonly called garnet yams.

you will need

Measuring spoons, vegetable peeler, chef's knife, medium bowl, baking sheet, oven mitt

ingredients

1 medium sweet potato

1 tablespoon olive oil

¾ teaspoon coarse salt

¼ teaspoon paprika

preparation

1 Preheat the oven to 425°F.

2 Using a vegetable peeler, peel the sweet potato. Using a chef's knife, cut it in half, **crosswise**. Stand one piece up, with a flat side on a cutting board, and cut ¼-inch slices. (Remember to use "the claw" to protect your fingers.) Stack the slices and cut them into fries, about ½ inch wide. Repeat the process with the rest of the potato.

3 Put the cut potatoes in a medium bowl, drizzle with the olive oil, and, with clean hands, toss until they are coated with oil. Add the salt and paprika and toss them again by gently shaking the bowl back and forth a few times. Arrange the potatoes on a baking sheet in one layer; do not crowd them, or they will not crisp.

4 **Bake** until the edges are browned and the fries look crisp, not moist, about 15 minutes. If the edges are not yet browned, bake for another 5 to 10 minutes. If the fries are very uneven in size, remove the baking sheet from the oven after 10 minutes—use an oven mitt!—and quickly give them a stir. Return the baking sheet to the oven and continue cooking until the fries are lightly browned. Turn off the oven and transfer the baking sheet to the countertop.

5 Let the fries cool for 2 to 3 minutes (but no more!). Serve warm.

Try dipping these
in the pesto from
page.49!

Makes 10 flatbreads

PAN-FRIED FLATBREADS WITH SPICED BUTTER

Soft, airy flatbreads are fun to make and even better to eat. There's a reason so many countries enjoy flatbreads every day—they cook much faster than loaf breads, so they can be whipped up last minute to go along with any meal, and they are made for wrapping, scooping, and sopping up the best, last bits on the plate. With homemade spice butter, they make a great snack all on their own.

you will need

Measuring cups, measuring spoons, 2 bowls, small spoon, medium bowl, whisk, wooden spoon, clean kitchen towel, baking sheet, parchment paper, rolling pin, griddle or heavy skillet, spatula, large plate

ingredients

FOR THE SPICED BUTTER

¼ cup unsalted butter

¾ teaspoon coarse salt

½ teaspoon ground turmeric

½ teaspoon ground cumin

½ teaspoon paprika or chile powder

preparation

Make the spiced butter

1 Cut the butter into small cubes and set them in a bowl on the counter to soften.

2 In a second bowl, combine the salt, turmeric, cumin, and paprika and mix until they are blended. Mix the spices into the softened butter with a small spoon.

CONTINUED

FOR THE FLATBREAD

1 cup all-purpose flour, plus more for dusting

½ cup whole-wheat flour

½ teaspoon baking powder

¼ teaspoon sugar

Coarse salt

¾ cup water

3 tablespoons Greek yogurt

1 tablespoon olive oil

Make the flatbread

1　In a medium bowl, whisk together the 1 cup all-purpose flour, whole-wheat flour, baking powder, sugar, and ½ teaspoon salt. Make a **well** in the middle and pour in the water, yogurt, and olive oil. Mix in the wet ingredients with a wooden spoon, then, with clean hands, bring the dough together and form it into a ball.

2　**Dust** ½ teaspoon all-purpose flour over a cutting board. Put the dough on the cutting board and **knead** it for 2 minutes. (Work your bread muscles! Press firmly with the heel of your hand into the dough, pushing it away from you.) If the dough sticks to your hands, lightly dust your hands with flour. When the dough is smooth, put it back in the bowl, cover it with a damp clean kitchen towel and let rest at room temperature for 30 minutes.

3　Line a baking sheet with parchment paper.

4　Break off a golf ball–size piece of the dough and roll it into a ball. On a clean cutting board, use a rolling pin to flatten the ball to about a ⅛-inch thickness—about as thick as a quarter. Rotate the bread a half turn after each roll to keep the shape round. If the dough sticks, dust the rolling pin with a **pinch** of flour. Repeat with the rest of the dough. As the breads are rolled out, set them onto the prepared baking sheet, side by side.

5　Heat an ungreased griddle to 350°F (or a heavy skillet to high). Drop a bead of water in the pan; if the water sizzles and evaporates (disappears), the pan is ready.

6　Using a spatula, add the breads two or three at a time and cook until a few brown spots appear and small bubbles of air form in the dough, about 1 minute per side. Transfer to a large plate and, once all the breads are fried, turn off the stove.

7　Serve the flatbreads warm, with a generous smear of spiced butter and an extra sprinkle of salt.

TIP

This dough doesn't need to rise, but it does need time to rest—this important step gives the flour time to absorb moisture from the water and yogurt, so even if you're feeling impatient, don't skip it!

We should first find someone to eat and drink with before we find something to eat and drink.

—EPICURUS

CHAPTER 4
SOMETHING TO DRINK

Watermelon Refresher (Agua de Sandia) 96

Orange-Lemon-Lime Fizz 99

Sparkling Mint Limeade 100

Creamy Dreamy Almond Milk 103

Strawberry-Almond Milk Shake 104

Mango Lassi 107

Mint Leaf Tea 108

Warm Masala Chai 111

A World of Spice 112

Perfect Hot Chocolate 114

Old-Fashioned Ginger Ale 117

WATERMELON REFRESHER (AGUA DE SANDIA)

Is it possible that watermelon is even better to drink than it is to eat? Zap it up in a blender—which takes about 1 minute—and even the least-great watermelon turns into a slushy, foamy, cooling delight. *Agua de sandia,* which means "water of watermelon," is a type of *agua fresca*—a Mexican drink made of fresh fruit pureed with water—that cleverly uses ripe fruit to beat the summer heat.

you will need

Measuring cup, chef's knife, small spoon, large serving spoon, blender

ingredients

2 limes

One 3- to 4-pound ripe watermelon

1½ cups water

A pinch of coarse salt

Ice cubes for serving

preparation

1   Using a knife, carefully cut one lime in half and cut the other lime into quarters.

2   Cut the watermelon in half. With the cut side down, quarter the watermelon and then remove the seeds with a small spoon. Cut the melon from the rind with a large serving spoon, scooping away from you. Roughly **chop** the melon (remember to use "the claw" to protect your fingers); you should have about 6 cups.

3   In a blender, combine the watermelon, water, and salt. Juice the lime halves into the blender. (**Reserve** the lime quarters for **garnish**.) **Blend,** starting on low speed and gradually working up to the highest setting, until smooth and **frothy**, about 30 seconds, then let it settle for a minute or so.

4   Serve in tall glasses over ice, with a squeeze of lime juice, if you like, and a quarter of lime for garnish.

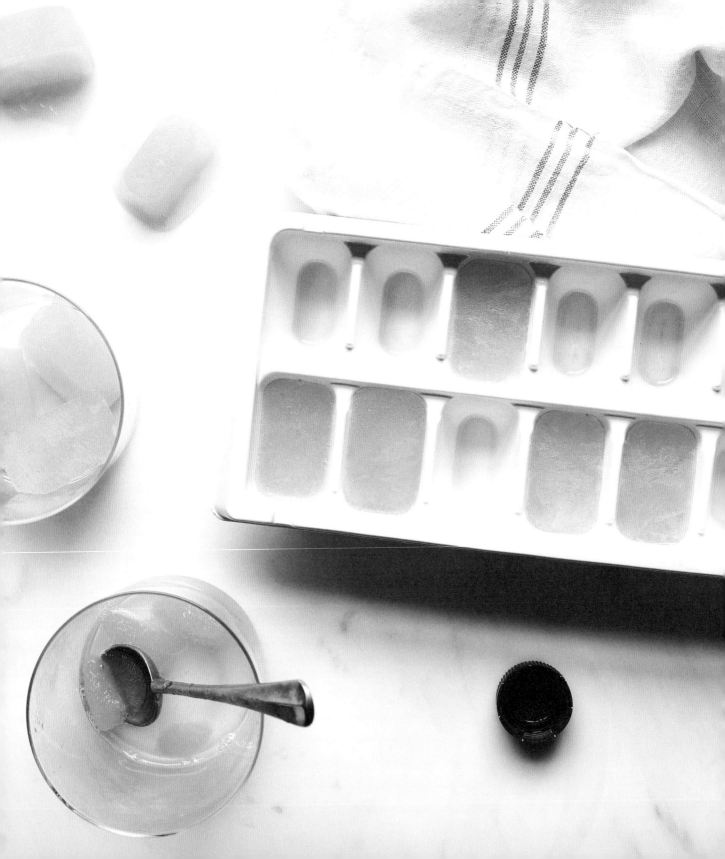

ORANGE-LEMON-LIME FIZZ

This fizzy fancy tonic is as easy as 1-2-3! Juice some oranges, lemons, and limes. Freeze the juice in an ice-cube tray. Add the fruity ice cubes to soda water and drink it up. For an extra treat, crunch on the tart, slushy ice left at the bottom of the glass.

you will need

Measuring cup, fine-mesh strainer, pitcher, knife, clean ice-cube tray, butter knife

ingredients

2 navel oranges

2 lemons

2 limes

4 cups sparkling water

preparation

1 Place a fine-mesh strainer over a pitcher.

2 Turn all the fruits onto their sides, so the stems face to the side, and slice in half. Juice the fruit into the strainer to remove any seeds. Stir the juice, then pour it into a clean ice-cube tray. Freeze until solid, about 2 hours.

3 Run a butter knife around the edges of the cubes to pop them from the tray. Put three cubes into each glass, add about 1 cup of the sparkling water, and stir until the ice begins to fizz.

4 Drink up.

DID YOU KNOW?

Why is citrus peel bitter? Self-defense! Birds and other animals aren't inspired to make their way through that bitter exterior to find the sweet fruit inside. But the squirrels in my neighborhood have gotten smart. When my tangerine tree is full of fruit, I'll often find a half-eaten one on our backyard table, the entire peel piled neatly next to it.

SPARKLING MINT LIMEADE

Limeade—lemonade's more fascinating cousin—crushes a big thirst like nothing else. Part of the citrus family, along with oranges, lemons, grapefruit, and others, limes can pickle, preserve, and enhance all kinds of foods because they are very acidic (that's what gives citrus its famously tart taste). If you don't have sparkling water on hand, tap water will work as long as you serve it with lots of ice.

you will need

Measuring cups, 2 small bowls, large pitcher, chef's knife, mortar and pestle or wooden spoon

ingredients

5 limes

1⅓ cups tap water

¼ cup sugar

Coarse salt

A few sprigs fresh mint, washed and patted dry

2 cups unflavored sparkling water or still water

preparation

1 On a cutting board, cut the limes in half, then squeeze the juice into a small bowl.

2 In a large pitcher, combine the tap water, 5 teaspoons of the sugar, a **pinch** of salt, and ⅔ cup of the lime juice. Stir until the sugar and salt have dissolved.

3 Pull about 15 mint leaves off the stems and roughly **chop** (unevenly, into bite-size pieces; remember to use "the claw" to protect your fingers). Place half of the chopped mint leaves into a mortar (if using), add 2½ teaspoons sugar, and crush with the pestle until nearly a paste. No mortar? Chop the mint finely, combine it with the sugar in a small bowl, and crush it with the back of a wooden spoon until the mint leaves start to break down.

4 Measure 1 tablespoon of the water-lime mixture into the mortar and stir it up to gather the mint and sugar from the sides of the bowl, then pour it into the pitcher. Crush the remaining sugar and mint in the mortar in the same way and add to the pitcher. (Taste the mixture—if it's too sour yet, stir in more sugar by the ¼ teaspoon, tasting after each addition, until it's as sweet as you like.)

5 When you're ready to serve the limeade, add the sparkling water to the pitcher and stir well.

TIP

To choose a juicy citrus, pick several fruits of the same size. Hold them in the palm of your hand one at a time. Choose the fruit that feels the heaviest for its size; this one has the most juice inside. Use this method for selecting pomegranates, too.

NOTE

If you don't have cheesecloth,
just use a fine-mesh strainer
and rinse it between each batch.

CREAMY DREAMY ALMOND MILK

Fresh almond milk is naturally sweeter than dairy milk, and creamier, too. Use it everywhere you would use regular milk or soy milk—it makes the best shakes, hands-down, and it's tops with granola and fresh fruit. *The hardest part is waiting for the almonds to soak overnight*—after that this recipe is done in 5 minutes flat.

you will need

Measuring cups, large bowl, blender, fine-mesh strainer, pitcher, cheesecloth, clean 2-cup (or larger) glass jar with tightly fitting lid

ingredients

½ cup whole raw almonds (skin on or **blanched**)

4 cups water

preparation

1　*At least 24 hours or up to a day and a half before you plan to serve,* put the almonds in a large bowl, add 2 cups of the water (**to cover**), and put in the refrigerator. After the almonds have soaked, **drain** and rinse them.

2　In a blender, combine the almonds with the remaining 2 cups water. **Blend**, starting on low speed and gradually working up to the highest setting, until the water has turned milky white and the almonds are ground fine, like sand, about 1 minute. This may take 30 seconds longer with a low-power blender.

3　**Strain** the almond milk in three batches. Place a fine-mesh strainer over a pitcher and line with cheesecloth (see Note). Gather up the edges of the cheesecloth to form a ball and twist gently to squeeze the ball. Discard the solids between each batch.

4　Pour the almond milk into a 2-cup glass jar. Rinse the strainer and the bowl and strain the liquid back and forth between the bowl and the jar a few more times, until the almond milk is smooth and there is just a little almond meal left at the bottom. Strain into the glass jar once more and cover with the lid.

5　The milk will keep, refrigerated, for up to 3 days. Almond milk will naturally separate (the solids from the liquid) in the refrigerator; give it a good stir before you use it.

STRAWBERRY-ALMOND MILK SHAKE

Fresh almond milk is a wonderful thing unto itself—creamy and dreamy! Mixed with sweet, fresh strawberries, this shake is *de-luscious*. For maximum creaminess, use homemade almond milk or opt for whole milk instead. And for the best flavor, use ripe strawberries at the peak of their growing season. Look for berries that are deep red, with no white spots.

you will need

Measuring cup, measuring spoons, paring knife, blender

ingredients

1 pint fresh strawberries

1 ripe (but not overripe!) banana

2 cups Creamy Dreamy Almond Milk (page 103) or whole milk

2 teaspoons honey, or **to taste**

3 ice cubes

preparation

1 Hull (remove the green stems and leaves from) the strawberries and cut the berries in half. Peel and slice the banana.

2 In a blender, combine the fruit, almond milk, honey, and ice. **Blend**, starting on low speed and gradually working up to the highest setting, until there are no visible chunks of fruit and the liquid turns pink, about 30 seconds. Taste and adjust the flavor with more honey, if needed. Stir again, and pour into tall glasses.

3 Serve immediately.

MANGO LASSI

This delectable mango "shake," traditional in India, combines rich, silky mango with tart yogurt for a surprisingly new flavor that's more sassy than sweet. It's thick, cooling, and filling—great for breakfast or a snack, but best for dessert. For the most flavor, choose very ripe mangos, either the Ataulfo or Alfonso variety. Next time you're in an Indian restaurant, order a mango lassi to get a taste of the real thing!

you will need

Measuring cup, measuring spoons, chef's knife, blender, long-handled spoon, fine-mesh strainer

ingredients

2 whole ripe mangos (see Note)

1 cup plain whole-milk yogurt

¼ cup water

5 ice cubes

½ tablespoon sugar, or to taste

A tiny **pinch** of coarse salt

A pinch of ground cardamom (optional)

preparation

1 **Chop** the mango into cubes (see page 76); you should have about 1 cup.

2 In a blender, combine the chopped mango, yogurt, water, ice cubes, sugar, salt, and cardamom (if using). Make sure the lid is fitted tightly onto the blender. **Blend**, starting on low speed and gradually working up to the highest setting. Count to 20. Turn off the blender and use a long-handled spoon to check the consistency and taste; the lassi should be thick and smooth, with no chunks of ice. Add an additional ¼ to ½ teaspoon sugar, if needed, and return the lid to blend again if it's not yet smooth.

3 **Strain** through a fine-mesh strainer into tall glasses.

NOTE

Mangoes are generally available year-round because they are imported from several countries with different growing seasons.

MINT LEAF TEA

Here is the simplest, most flavorful tea—made from nothing more than boiling water poured over a handful of fresh mint. If you can find (or plant!) Persian mint, do. It's sweeter and more fragrant than spearmint and it makes the best-tasting tea with an otherworldly golden-green hue.

you will need

Measuring cup, knife, teapot or large ceramic bowl, kettle or small saucepan, wooden spoon

ingredients

1 bunch fresh mint

3 cups water

Honey for serving (optional)

preparation

1 Rinse the mint and shake it to remove excess water. Place the whole bunch on a cutting board and cut off the stems. Place the mint leaves in a teapot (a large ceramic bowl will also work).

2 In a kettle or small saucepan over high heat, bring the 3 cups water to a **boil**. Then, turn off the stove, pour the boiling water over the leaves, and press down with a wooden spoon to fully submerge them—the hot water prevents them from **oxidizing** (turning brown).

3 **Steep** for 3 minutes and then **strain** into mugs.

4 Serve hot, with a spoonful of honey per cup, if desired. Mint tea can also be chilled and served cold.

WARM MASALA CHAI

Chai, a sweet and fragrant milky tea from India, is the perfect foil for a winter-morning chill, and a treat any time of year. As it steeps, an aromatic blend of honey and spice infuse the milk—and your kitchen—with the intoxicating scent of ginger, cardamom, and vanilla. In India, chai is dispensed from small carts on nearly every corner, a daily cup of warmth.

you will need

Measuring cup, measuring spoons, paring knife, large saucepan, fine-mesh strainer

ingredients

1-inch piece fresh ginger

8 cardamom pods or ¼ teaspoon ground cardamom

1 small cinnamon stick

½ teaspoon black peppercorns

½ teaspoon fennel seeds (optional)

½ vanilla bean

2½ cups whole milk

½ cup water

1 tablespoon honey

1 bag decaffeinated black tea

preparation

1. Cut the ginger into thick (about ¼-inch) slices—no need to peel it.

2. In a large saucepan, combine the cardamom, cinnamon, peppercorns, fennel seeds (if using), and vanilla bean. Set over low heat and warm until fragrant, 30 to 45 seconds.

3. Add the milk, water, and sliced ginger to the saucepan, turn the heat to medium-high, and bring to a low **boil**. As soon as it begins to boil, turn the heat to medium-low, and **simmer** gently for 2 minutes.

4. Stir the honey into the pan. Remove any tag from the tea bag and drop the whole bag into the milk. Turn off the stove, cover the pot, and let the tea **steep** for 10 minutes.

5. **Strain** the chai through a fine-mesh strainer directly into mugs.

6. Serve immediately.

DID YOU KNOW?

The terms "herb" and "spice" refer to separate parts of the plant. An *herb* is used fresh, and consists of the leaves and stalks of the plant (such as dill or basil). A *spice* is dried and consists of the bud, flower, seed, root, berry, or bark of the plant (such as ginger or cinnamon).

A WORLD OF SPICE

Herbs and spices have been treasured for thousands of years. These are just a few (of many!) that transform food from so-so to super delicious.

CINNAMON

Cinnamon "sticks" are actually shaved pieces of cinnamon tree bark! The story goes that giant birds once built their nests from cinnamon sticks. To trick the birds, spice traders left whole, slaughtered cows in the canyon below. When the birds brought "dinner" home, the nest cracked to pieces, sending cinnamon sticks tumbling down the mountain, to be snatched up by the clever traders.

PEPPER

Black, white, and green peppercorns are the tiny fruit of a bushy vine originally from India. Black pepper is picked before it's ripe, then dried into a tough wrinkly orb. At one time, this spice was so valuable that people paid their taxes and rent in peppercorns!

VANILLA

This very special little pod—technically a fruit—grows on a beautiful orchid plant. Inside the pod are thousands of tiny, fragrant seeds. The flower blossoms for only a few hours and *never opens again*, so if bees miss their chance to pollinate, no fruit can grow. One day a young boy named Edmund Albius discovered he could hand-pollinate the flowers. Thanks to Edmund, commercial growers can now produce lots of vanilla, by pollinating—and harvesting—each flower by hand.

GINGER

I always thought ginger was a root, but guess what? It's actually a rhizome—a stem that grows underground and sends out shoots and roots from its sides. Originally a medicine, ginger was eventually mixed with ale and cake to cure stomach aches—the first ginger ale and gingerbread! Back then, a pound of ginger was worth a whole live sheep! Today, the world grows more than *two million tons* of ginger every year.

CARDAMOM

Exotic, aromatic cardamom—a cousin to ginger—has been a flavoring and medicine for over *four thousand years*! Crush open the pod and inhale—the smell is intoxicating! Inside, you'll find dozens of soft little seeds. Both parts—seed and pod—are used in cooking. Eat the seeds, but discard whole pods before serving; they're just there to perfume the dish.

PERFECT HOT CHOCOLATE

Extra-thick and chocolatey, this hot chocolate is a riff on a recipe that's thousands of years old—really! The Aztecs mixed chocolate with spices such as chile and vanilla and drank it during special ceremonies as an elixir for strength and vitality. Here is a rich version that captures all the chocolate essence without the spicy kick.

you will need

Measuring cup, measuring spoons, small bowl, medium saucepan, whisk

ingredients

2½ ounces semisweet chocolate

¼ teaspoon ground cinnamon or 1 whole cinnamon stick

2 tablespoons light brown sugar

2 cups whole milk

A **pinch** of salt

preparation

1 Break the chocolate into small pieces and set aside. If using ground cinnamon, combine it with the brown sugar in a small bowl and mix well.

2 In a medium saucepan over medium heat, bring the milk to a gentle **simmer**, whisking constantly. Stir in the chocolate, salt, and brown sugar (and add the cinnamon stick, if using). Whisk until the sugar dissolves and the chocolate melts. Turn the heat to medium-high, until the milk is at a vigorous simmer, and cook for another 2 minutes, whisking until the milk becomes **frothy** (air bubbles cover the top of the milk). Turn off the stove.

3 Pour the hot chocolate into mugs (fish out the cinnamon stick) and allow to cool for a moment. The mixture should have the thickness of heavy whipping cream. Serve hot.

DID YOU KNOW?

The botanical name for chocolate, *Theobroma cacao*, translates to "food of the gods." For good reason, don't you think?

VARIATION

For even more chocolatey goodness, add another
2 ounces chocolate and 1 tablespoon brown sugar.
Or, for a little less sweetness, decrease the sugar
to 1 tablespoon plus 2 teaspoons.

TIP

If you like your ginger ale with a little more zip, use an extra half inch of fresh ginger.

OLD-FASHIONED GINGER ALE

Ginger and lime are like a dynamic duo of "root" and fruit. Ginger turns the sour limes sweet, and limes calm that spicy ginger edge until it's got just the right amount of zip. To make the ginger ale, you'll start with a simple syrup—a sweetener made by boiling sugar and water together—then add fresh raw ginger for flavor. Simple syrups can be flavored with nearly anything! Mix it up with bubbly water and lime luice and your ginger ale is good to go!

you will need

Measuring cups, paring knife, small bowl, medium pot, blender, fine-mesh strainer, pitcher, wooden spoon

ingredients

4 limes

4 ounces fresh ginger (a roughly 3-inch-long by 1-inch-wide piece)

¾ cup tap water

¾ cup sugar

One 1-liter bottle unflavored sparkling water, cold

Ice cubes for serving

preparation

1   Cut the limes in half and then juice them into a small bowl; you should have ½ cup of juice.

2   Wash the ginger thoroughly (break apart the pieces to wash in between); no need to peel it. Cut into ½-inch-thick slices.

3   In a medium pot, combine the chopped ginger, tap water, and sugar. Place over high heat and bring to a rolling **boil**, about 3 minutes. When the mixture comes to a boil, turn the heat to low and **simmer** for 10 minutes. Turn off the stove and allow the mixture to cool for 5 minutes.

4   Pour the mixture, including the ginger pieces, into a blender and fit the lid on tightly. **Blend**, starting on low speed and gradually working up to the highest setting. Count to 20, then turn off the blender. The pieces of ginger should be very small (roly-poly-size or smaller). If not, replace the lid and blend again for another count of 10.

5   Put a fine-mesh strainer over a pitcher and then **strain** the mixture into the pitcher. Press the ginger against the strainer with a wooden spoon to extract any remaining liquid, then discard the ginger. Mix the lime juice and sparkling water into the pitcher and stir well. Taste, and adjust the flavor with more lime juice or sparkling water, if needed.

6   Serve over ice.

One of the very nicest things about life is the way we must regularly stop whatever it is we are doing and devote our attention to eating.

—LUCIANO PAVAROTTI

CHAPTER 5

WHAT'S FOR DINNER?

Super-Simple Side Salad 120

Vinaigrettes: Basic Vinaigrette
and Garlic Vinaigrette 122

Two-Minute Green Beans 125

Salty Roasty Potatoes 126

Marble-Size Meatballs with
Quick and Easy Tomato Sauce 129

Crispy Skillet Chicken 132

Warm and Cozy Sausage Soup 134

Home-Cooked White Beans 137

SUPER-SIMPLE SIDE SALAD

Salads can be anything you like—filling or light, tart and tangy, rich and creamy—it's up to you. To make a great salad, all you really need is a vegetable or two—or a fruit for that matter—and a tasty dressing. Here's a basic recipe with a couple of dressings to get you started. Make sure your salad greens are well dried before dressing them. Because oil and water don't mix, the oil in the dressing won't stick to wet leaves. If you're not sure of the best way to dive in to a big bowl of salad, try "stackers," my son Jasper's secret salad technique: stack all the toppings on a single lettuce leaf and eat it like a crunchy open-faced sandwich.

you will need

Paring knife, vegetable peeler, large bowl

ingredients

2 carrots

1 cucumber

½-ounce piece Parmesan cheese

1 small head red leaf or butter lettuce, washed and dried

1 recipe vinaigrette (see page 123)

Coarse salt

Ground black pepper

preparation

1 Cut the ends off the carrots and cucumber and throw them away. Peel them, discard the peel, and shave into long ribbons with a vegetable peeler. Shave the Parmesan cheese into ribbons with the peeler.

2 In a large bowl, toss together the lettuce, carrots, and cucumber. Pour some of the vinaigrette over and toss the salad again to coat it with dressing. Taste a small bite and adjust the amount of salt, pepper, and vinaigrette if needed. Heap the salad onto plates or into bowls and top with the Parmesan ribbons.

3 Serve immediately.

 **VARIATION**

Add any one, or a combination, of toppings

* Sliced, fresh radish, celery, fennel, or snap peas or quartered tomatoes
* Hard-boiled eggs (see page 44), grilled chicken, or cooked fish
* 1 tablespoon chopped assorted herbs, such as mint, parsley, tarragon, or dill

HOW TO WASH AND DRY LETTUCE

Fill the outside bowl of a salad spinner with cold water. Pull the lettuce leaves one by one from the stem and drop them into the water. Swish the leaves around with your hand several times. Loosen the dirt with your fingers, if needed. Swish a few more times.

Wait a few minutes while the dirt settles to the bottom of the bowl. Lift the greens gently from the water so the dirt stays on the bottom and drain the water. Shake off the excess water from the greens and put them in the salad spinner. Spin a few times, discard the water, then spin again. Move the lettuce to a clean towel and pat it dry.

If you don't have a salad spinner, rinse the lettuce in a large bowl of water, **drain** it, and lay it out on a clean dishcloth. Pat it dry with a second cloth.

Gather the corners of the first cloth, twist them into a tail, and shake the lettuce gently from side to side to remove excess water. Pat again until the lettuce is dry.

VINAIGRETTES

Vinaigrettes are a thick, cloudy **emulsion** (a combination of liquids that are normally unmixable—like oil and water); and they are "unstable emulsions" because, pretty quickly after blending, they separate again. So we often add things to build a bridge between the oil and vinegar, like mashed garlic, mustard, and mayonnaise. These are called *emulsifiers* because they bind the oil and vinegar together.

To make a vinaigrette, always start with the vinegar. Measure it into a small bowl and then add salt and any other flavorings (herbs, garlic, pepper, mustard). Stir with a whisk or fork until the salt dissolves. The salt can't dissolve in the oil, so adding it to the vinegar is a way to make sure the flavor is in all parts of the dressing. *Sloooowly* add the oil next, whisking as you go, to *emulsify* the dressing.

BASIC VINAIGRETTE

Makes ½ cup

you will need

Measuring cup, measuring spoons, small bowl, whisk

ingredients

2 tablespoons red or white wine vinegar

½ teaspoon coarse salt

A **pinch** of ground black pepper

¼ cup plus 2 tablespoons olive oil

preparation

1 In a small bowl, whisk together the vinegar, salt, and pepper.

2 Very slowly pour the olive oil into the bowl in one steady stream, whisking the entire time. The dressing will form an **emulsion** and become cloudy. If the oil and vinegar are still separate after a lot of whisking, put the mixture in a glass jar with a tight-fitting lid and shake it really well. Vinaigrette will keep in a sealed glass jar in the refrigerator for up to 3 days. Whisk well before using.

GARLIC VINAIGRETTE

Makes ½ cup

you will need

Measuring cup, measuring spoons, mortar and pestle, whisk

ingredients

1 garlic clove (see Note)

Coarse salt

3 tablespoons red or white wine vinegar

Ground black pepper

⅓ cup olive oil

preparation

1 Trim the **stem end** from the garlic, and smash the clove with a pestle. Put half the garlic and a **pinch** of salt in a mortar and pound to a paste. (Save the other half for another recipe or discard.)

2 Add the vinegar, a pinch of pepper, and another very small pinch of salt to the garlic and stir to mix. Slowly pour the olive oil into the mortar in one steady stream, whisking constantly, until the dressing emulsifies. Vinaigrette will keep in a sealed glass jar in the refrigerator for up to 3 days. Whisk well before using.

NOTE

If you don't have a mortar and pestle, **mince** the garlic and crush it in a small bowl with the back of a wooden spoon.

TWO-MINUTE GREEN BEANS

Clocking in at about 2 minutes **prep** time, sweet and snappy green beans
are hands-down the freshest, easiest side dish you can make. The beans are
blanched (cooked in salty, boiling water for just a moment) so they keep their
color and crunch. For the most flavor, look for smaller beans that are smooth
and firm, with just a little bit of shine.

you will need

Measuring cup, measuring
spoons, large pot, colander,
paring knife

ingredients

Coarse salt

1 pound green beans

A few sprigs (about 10 leaves)
fresh basil or mint, or both

2 tablespoons olive oil

1 tablespoon red or
white wine vinegar

A **pinch** or two of ground
black pepper

preparation

1 Fill a large pot with 6 cups water and 2 tablespoons salt. Cover,
place over high heat, and bring to a rolling **boil**. While the water is
heating, snap (and discard) the **stem end** from each green bean.
Set a colander into the sink.

2 When the water is boiling, drop in the beans and cook, uncovered,
for 1 minute. *If the beans are much wider than your pinky finger,
cook for 2 minutes.* Turn off the stove and immediately **drain** the
beans in the colander and rinse with very cold water for a minute
to keep them from overcooking.

3 Pull the basil leaves from the stems. Stack the leaves and, using a
small knife, **chiffonade** (roll into a pencil shape and thinly slice them).

4 Arrange the cooked green beans on a serving dish. Drizzle the olive oil
and vinegar over them and sprinkle with a pinch of salt and pepper.
Toss the basil over the top.

5 Serve warm or at room temperature.

SALTY ROASTY POTATOES

If you like your potatoes with perfectly crispy fried skin on the outside and steamy-creamy soft insides, you're in luck! It's that same mix of sweet and crunch that probably earned potatoes their French name, *pommes de terre*—"earth apples." Roasted potatoes round out any meal of meat or fish and make a simple salad feel like a feast.

you will need

Measuring spoons, chef's knife, small spoon, medium bowl, baking sheet, fork

ingredients

1 pound small round potatoes (golf ball–size or smaller)

2 sprigs fresh rosemary or thyme

2 large garlic cloves

2 tablespoons olive oil

¾ teaspoon coarse salt

preparation

1 Preheat the oven to 425°F.

2 Rinse and thoroughly dry the potatoes and then cut them into quarters. Pull the leaves from the herbs and **chop** them finely (the size of ants; remember to use "the claw" to protect your fingers). Trim and discard the root end from the garlic and smash once with the back of a spoon; remove the peel.

3 In a medium bowl, combine the potatoes and olive oil and mix together until the potatoes are well coated. Sprinkle in the salt, chopped herbs, and smashed garlic and mix again. Pour the potatoes onto a baking sheet in one layer.

4 **Roast** until the potatoes are browned at the edges, 25 to 30 minutes. Stab the largest one with a fork to make sure it's tender. If not, cook for another 5 minutes and test again. Remove from the oven, turn off the oven, and let potatoes coolon the baking sheet for a full 5 minutes.

5 Serve warm!

VARIATION

For breakfast or lunch, serve up a bowl of roasted potatoes with a fried egg on top.

MARBLE-SIZE MEATBALLS WITH QUICK AND EASY TOMATO SAUCE

The secret to super-moist meatballs is a handful of milky bread crumbs and Parmesan cheese in the mix. In Italy, meatballs are called *polpetti,* and they are served on their own, or with a simple tomato sauce. (You read that right: No spaghetti!). At home, Italians eat an even *smaller* kind called *polpettine,* about the size of marbles—small enough to eat in one bite!

you will need

Measuring cups, measuring spoons, chef's knife, 2 small bowls, small spoon, large bowl, box grater, baking sheet, ladle

ingredients

A few sprigs fresh marjoram or oregano

2 thick slices rustic-style bread

1/4 cup whole milk

1 egg

1 pound ground beef

1/2 teaspoon coarse salt

Ground black pepper

1 small garlic clove

1/2 cup grated Parmesan or Pecorino Romano cheese, plus more for serving

1 teaspoon Dijon mustard

1 recipe Quick and Easy Tomato Sauce (page 131), warm

preparation

1 Preheat the oven to 425°F.

2 **Chop** the marjoram leaves into the size of ladybugs (remember to use "the claw" to protect your fingers) and **reserve** a heaping 2 teaspoons.

3 Remove the crusts from the bread, then break the bread into bite-size pieces. Measure 1½ cups bread pieces (loosely **packed**) and put into a small bowl. Pour the milk over the bread and then push down so all of it gets soaked. In a second bowl, crack the egg and then remove any shell with a small spoon.

4 In a large bowl, combine the beef, ¼ teaspoon of the salt, and 4 pinches of pepper. Grate the garlic into the meat, using the smallest holes of a box grater; use the spoon to sweep any leftover garlic from inside the grater. Add the egg, cheese, mustard, and herbs to the beef and mix together by hand.

5 Check the bread; break it up by hand into very small (roly-poly-size) pieces and mix it well with the milk. If needed, add a few more bite-size pieces of bread until there is no more milk at the bottom of the bowl. Mix the soaked bread into the meat, breaking up any bigger pieces.

CONTINUED

6 Form meatballs by rolling the meat between the palms of your hands into a round shape. For polpettine (marble-size), use 2 teaspoons of meat for each one; for polpetti (golf ball–size), use 2 tablespoons of meat. Arrange the meatballs on a baking sheet in one, uncrowded layer.

7 **Bake** until cooked through, 8 to 10 minutes for polpettine or 12 to 15 minutes for polpetti. When you think they are done, cut one open to make sure they are fully cooked! The meat should be brown all the way through. When the meatballs are cooked, turn off the oven.

8 Ladle a big scoop of tomato sauce into a shallow bowl, top with 6 meatballs, and sprinkle with grated Parmesan cheese.

9 Serve while it's nice and warm.

WHAT HAPPENS IF THE GARLIC STARTS TO BROWN?

Garlic is both friend and foe to a cook! It can make your food extra-tasty, but when it burns, it turns *bitter*. The smaller the garlic (like minced) the faster it cooks, so keep a close watch. If the garlic is sizzling, it's cooking too fast—add the other ingredients, stir, and quickly lower the heat. If the garlic is turning brown, and you smell a faint burnt smell, it's best to clean out the pan and start again.

QUICK AND EASY TOMATO SAUCE

You may know this traditional tomato sauce as *marinara*—Italian for "sailor sauce." Maybe it's called that because the sailors knew a thing or two about good cooking? Whatever the reason, this simple sauce is proof that tomatoes were meant for garlic and olive oil, and when they're cooked all together, you can hardly go wrong. Pour over your favorite pasta, meat, or thickly sliced grilled bread and season with a drizzle of olive oil and salt and pepper, if you like.

If you're making the sauce to pair with meatballs, make the meatballs first and reheat them in the sauce just before serving.

you will need

Measuring spoons, paring knife, medium bowl, deep wide (12-inch or larger) skillet, wooden spoon, blender

ingredients

6 garlic cloves

One 28-ounce can whole peeled tomatoes

5 tablespoons olive oil, plus more for **garnish**

Coarse salt

A few pinches of ground black pepper

1 sprig fresh basil

preparation

1 Trim and discard both ends of each garlic clove. Peel and slice the garlic into thin slivers, about as thick as a quarter.

2 Pour the tomatoes with all their juices into a medium bowl and, using your hands, crush them into small bite-size pieces. The sauce will be as thick and chunky as you make these pieces, so keep that in mind as you work.

3 Put 3 tablespoons of the olive oil in a deep, wide skillet and place over medium heat. Count to 15, add the garlic and a **pinch** of salt, and then stir. Let the garlic warm up and become fragrant—about 30 seconds—but don't let it brown. When you start to smell the garlic, pour in the tomatoes with all the juice.

4 Using a wooden spoon, stir in the remaining 2 tablespoons olive oil, ¾ teaspoon salt, the pepper, and basil (on the stem). Turn the heat to medium-high, bring to a **simmer**, cover, and cook for 15 minutes. Turn off the stove and fish out and discard the basil.

5 For smooth sauce, let it cool for 5 minutes, then transfer carefully to a blender and puree on low speed for 30 seconds, holding down the lid with a towel to prevent splattering. Tomato sauce can be stored in a tightly sealed container in the refrigerator for up to 3 days.

CRISPY SKILLET CHICKEN

This chicken is super-fun to make because you get to smack it with a frying pan. Flattening it out makes it cook *really* fast—about 5 minutes on each side. For extra-crispy chicken, ask the butcher for boneless pieces with the skin still on.

you will need

Measuring spoons, wax paper, large (12-inch) skillet, paring knife, small spoon, spatula

ingredients

2 small boneless chicken breasts (about 6 ounces each)

½ teaspoon coarse salt

2 pinches of ground black pepper

4 small garlic cloves

1 tablespoon olive oil

5 sprigs fresh thyme

5 sprigs fresh rosemary

TIP

The thicker the chicken is, the longer it takes to cook, so if you don't get it to ¼ inch, that's okay, but expect it to take a few more minutes to cook on each side.

preparation

1. Cut a large piece of wax paper, about the size of a sheet of binder paper. Lay it on a cutting board, fold it in half, and place the chicken inside, skin-side down. Close the paper over the chicken.

2. Pound the chicken with the bottom of a large skillet to flatten it to about ¼ inch thick. (Don't whack it too hard or it will tear.) Season it on both sides with ¼ teaspoon of the salt and the pepper.

3. Using a paring knife, trim and discard one end of each garlic clove; leave the peel on. Place the garlic on the cutting board and smash them with the back of a spoon—just enough to break them open.

4. Place the skillet over high heat and add the olive oil. Count to 20, then use a spatula to lay the chicken pieces in the pan, skin-side down. *Move your hands away quickly—the oil will sizzle and pop!* Add the garlic to the pan.

5. Cook the chicken until the skin crisps and browns, about 4 minutes. Using the spatula, lift the chicken to check the skin. If it's not golden brown, cook for another 1 to 2 minutes, then check again.

6. Once the skin is golden brown, add the thyme and rosemary to the pan. Using the spatula, flip the chicken to cook the other side, laying the pieces directly on top of the herbs. Cook for 4 minutes, then move the chicken from the pan to a plate.

7. Use the paring knife to make a small cut into the thickest part of each piece to check if it's fully cooked; the meat should be white all the way through, no pink showing. Cook another minute or so if needed. Turn off the stove. Eat while warm or at room temperature.

dinner is served!

WARM AND COZY SAUSAGE SOUP

In winter, when it gets dark really early, a thick and creamy bowl of soup with sausage and beans is just the thing for Sunday supper. Here's one you can make for your whole family in less than an hour, and all in one pot! For the most flavorful soup, use chicken stock instead of broth. The soup can be stored right in the pot you cooked it in, covered and refrigerated, for up to 3 days.

you will need

Measuring cup, measuring spoons, chef's knife, heavy stockpot or Dutch oven, long-handled spoon, 2 medium bowls, ladle, blender

ingredients

2 small garlic cloves

3 tablespoons extra-virgin olive oil

1 medium yellow or white onion

3 cups Home-Cooked White Beans (page 137) or two 16-ounce cans navy or cannellini beans

2 precooked sausages, such as mild or spicy Italian or smoked bratwurst

Coarse salt

Ground black pepper

2 cups chicken stock (not broth)

Thick slices of bread for serving

Parmesan cheese for serving

Handful of chopped fresh parsley for serving

preparation

1 Peel and finely **chop** the garlic, about the size of ants. (Remember to use "the claw" to protect your fingers.) **Dice** the onion (see page 138).

2 Add 1 tablespoon of the olive oil to a heavy stockpot or Dutch oven and place over medium heat. Count to 20. Add the garlic, stir a few times with a long-handled spoon, then add the onion and cook for 15 minutes. Stir every few minutes, until the onion is soft and melty. If it starts to brown, add 1 tablespoon water and lower the heat.

3 While the onion is cooking, **drain** and rinse the beans and set them aside in a medium bowl. Then, cut the sausage into ½-inch slices and put those in a second medium bowl. Once the onion has cooked for 15 minutes, add the sliced sausage and cook, stirring, for 3 minutes. Add the beans, a generous **pinch** of salt, and a pinch of pepper. Stir for a few minutes, add the chicken stock, bring to a **simmer**, and cook for 10 minutes.

4 Take a ladleful (about ½ cup) of the beans (with stock, but no meat) out of the pot and transfer to a blender. Make sure the lid is on tightly, and hold it down with a dish towel. **Blend**, starting on low speed and gradually working up to the highest setting. Count to 10. Pour the blended beans into the soup, add the remaining 2 tablespoons olive oil, and heat the soup for 5 minutes more. Taste and add more salt or pepper, if needed. Turn off the stove.

5 Serve warm, with thickly sliced bread, a heaping spoonful of Parmesan cheese, and a sprinkle of parsley.

VARIATIONS

For a little more zip, stir in 1 tablespoon of pesto (see page 49) at the end, or add ¼ teaspoon red pepper flakes to the onion while it is cooking.

To substitute bacon for sausage, chop 5 bacon slices and cook together with the onion for the full 15 minutes before adding the beans.

HOME-COOKED WHITE BEANS

White beans give a little extra love to all types of salads and soups. They are especially good mashed with sautéed garlic and salt and slathered on toast. Cooked beans will keep, covered and refrigerated, for up to 3 days.

you will need

Measuring cups, measuring spoons, medium bowl, stockpot

ingredients

1 cup dried white (cannellini) beans

1 small yellow or white onion, peeled and halved

1 bay leaf

A few sprigs fresh thyme

2 tablespoons olive oil

Coarse salt

preparation

1   *One day before you plan to serve,* put the beans in a medium bowl and add water **to cover** by 3 inches (this means, add enough water so the beans are covered and there is about 3 inches of water above the top of them), cover the bowl, and refrigerate it overnight.

2   The next day, **drain** and rinse the beans and put them in a stockpot with enough fresh water to cover by 4 inches.

3   Add the onion, bay leaf, and thyme to the beans and bring them to a rolling **boil** over high heat. Once the water is boiling, turn the heat to medium and **simmer**, uncovered, until the beans are tender but not falling apart, about 1 hour. Turn off the stove.

4   Let the beans cool in the pot with their cooking water. Once cooled, stir in the olive oil and ½ teaspoon salt. Taste a few beans and add salt by the **pinch**, as needed.

HOW TO DICE AN ONION

1.
Trim the stem end.

2.
Place the onion cut-side down and cut in half through the root end.

3.
Peel off the skin.

4.
FOR A LARGE DICE
Place the knife blade into the cut end of the
onion and slice very gently and slowly through
the middle, parallel to the cutting board and just
up to the root but not through it,
leaving the root intact.

5.
Rotate the onion so the root is facing away
from you. Drop the tip of the knife down gently
at the root end, as close as you can get without
cutting into the root. Slice all the way to the
opposite end of the onion; repeat, making
slices ½-inch apart.

6.
Rotate the onion again. Make slices
½-inch apart from the cut
side to the root.

TIP.

FOR A FINE DICE

Follow the steps for large dice,
but make the cuts closer together.

CHAPTER 6

SWEETS AND TREATS

Tangerine Snow 142

Raspberry Clouds 145

Ice Cream Monday 147

Monday Toppers: Nearly Fudge Chocolate Sauce,
Vanilla Whipped Cream, and Sweet and Salty
Candied Walnuts 148

Peach and Nectarine Crisp 150

Piece-of-Cake Lemon Cake 154

Chocolate Lava Cupcakes 157

Once in a young lifetime,
one should be allowed
to have as much sweetness
as one can possibly
want and hold.

—JUDITH OLNEY

TANGERINE SNOW

This fluffed ice treat, also known as *granita,* works with just about any fruit juice, but tangy tangerine is my all-time favorite. The hardest part is waiting for the granita to freeze. It takes about 2 hours, so plan on doing something fun to pass the time. Make it on a Saturday morning and you'll be treating yourself (and your friends) all afternoon.

you will need

Measuring cups, small bowl, medium saucepan, freezer-proof container (such as a glass pie dish or 2-quart baking dish), fork

ingredients

3 pounds tangerines

¾ cup water

½ cup granulated sugar

Handful of pomegranate seeds for topping (optional)

preparation

1 Clear a flat space in the freezer.

2 Juice the tangerines into a small bowl and remove any seeds. Measure out 1½ cups juice and **reserve**. (Drink the rest or refrigerate for another use.)

3 In a medium saucepan over a medium heat, combine the water and sugar and cook until the mixture comes to a **boil**. Turn off the stove.

4 Stir the tangerine juice into the pan and then allow to cool for several minutes.

5 Pour the juice into a freezer-proof container so it's just about ½ inch high in the dish. Carefully transfer the juice pan to the freezer and freeze, uncovered, for at least 2 hours or up to 2 days.

6 Just before serving, scrape back and forth across the ice with a fork to "fluff" it up into tiny crystals, like fresh snow. Spoon the granita quickly into glasses, top with pomegranate seeds, if desired, and eat before it melts!

THE ORIGINAL SWEET TOOTH

Scientists think our ancestors had a real "sweet tooth"—a taste for sweets and an instinct for finding them. In those days, "sweets" would have been juicy berries on the vine, honey still in the comb, and raw maple syrup literally coming out of the tree. That's pretty different than what we think of as sweets now, right?

RASPBERRY CLOUDS

Sometimes the best dessert is the easiest dessert. These raspberry clouds taste exactly like they sound, and take only a few minutes to make. In England, where this dreamy concoction is popular all summer long, they call this *Eton Mess*. And stirring ripe fruit into freshly whipped cream is messy business indeed! Clouds are equally heavenly with strawberries if no raspberries are available.

you will need

Measuring cup, measuring spoons, small bowl, wooden spoon, fork, small cup, medium bowl, whisk

ingredients

1 pint raspberries or strawberries

6 teaspoons sugar

2 or 3 meringues (see Note; optional)

1 cup heavy whipping cream

¼ teaspoon vanilla extract

preparation

1 In a small bowl, combine the raspberries and 3 teaspoons of the sugar and stir gently with a wooden spoon. Smash a few—but not all—of the raspberries into the sugar with the back of a fork. After 10 minutes, **drain** the sugary syrup that has formed at the bottom of the bowl into a small cup and **reserve**. If using strawberries, hull (remove the green stems and leaves from) the strawberries and cut the berries into quarters before adding the sugar. There is no need to smash the strawberries.

2 While the berries are soaking, crush the meringue (if using) into bite-size pieces.

3 In a medium bowl, combine the cream, vanilla, and remaining 3 teaspoons sugar. Using a whisk, **whip** the cream until it begins to stiffen slightly (the whisk will leave indentations in the cream), 5 to 8 minutes.

4 Add the berries to the whipped cream and stir gently with the wooden spoon.

5 Dish a small heap of "mess" (about ½ cup) into each bowl. Drizzle with 1 teaspoon of the reserved berry syrup, and top with a sprinkle of crushed meringue. Eat immediately!

NOTE

A meringue is a light, crunchy cookie made of whipped egg whites and sugar. They can be purchased at most bakeries and some supermarkets.

ICE CREAM MONDAY

I think ice cream should be for Mondays instead of Sundays. What better way to start the week off right! With scrumptious candied walnuts on top, your weeknight ice cream will feel like a super-sundae treat. Mix and match with fresh chocolate sauce and vanilla whipped cream . . . or save those for next Monday.

you will need

ice-cream scoop, small bowls

ingredients

4 scoops vanilla or chocolate ice cream, or both, if you please

Sweet and Salty Candied Walnuts (page 149) for serving

Nearly Fudge Chocolate Sauce (page 148) for serving

Vanilla Whipped Cream (page 148) for serving

preparation

1. Scoop the ice cream into small bowls and dress it up with a heaping spoonful of walnuts, a drizzle of chocolate sauce, and a dollop of whipped cream.

2. Serve immediately.

 TIP

For a sweet holiday gift, double the recipe for the candied walnuts and pack them into a mason jar with a colorful ribbon tied around the top.

MONDAY TOPPERS

NEARLY FUDGE CHOCOLATE SAUCE

Makes about 1 cup

you will need

Measuring cup, measuring spoons, knife, small bowl, small saucepan, wooden spoon, clean jar with a fitted lid

ingredients

4 ounces semisweet chocolate

¾ cup heavy whipping cream

2 tablespoons sugar

1 tablespoon butter

1 teaspoon vanilla extract

preparation

1   **Chop** the chocolate into small chunks about the size of large chocolate chips (remember to use "the claw" to protect your fingers) and put them into a small bowl.

2   In a small saucepan over low heat, combine the cream, sugar, and butter. Stir until the butter is melted and the sugar is completely dissolved, about 2 minutes. The moment you see bubbles at the edges of the pot, remove it from the heat and turn off the stove.

3   Pour the chocolate chunks into the warm cream and add the vanilla. Let the mixture sit for 2 minutes (don't stir it). After 2 minutes, stir until the mixture is smooth. Transfer to a clean jar with a fitted lid. Chocolate sauce will keep in the refrigerator for up to 1 week. It thickens as it cools; to bring it back to pourable consistency, put it in a double boiler and warm it over low heat.

VANILLA WHIPPED CREAM

you will need

Measuring cup, measuring spoons, large mixing bowl (stainless steel is best), whisk or electric mixer with whisk attachment

ingredients

½ cup heavy whipping cream

⅛ teaspoon vanilla extract

Makes about 1 cup

preparation

1   In a large mixing bowl, combine the cream and vanilla. With a whisk or electric mixer, **whip** the cream until it begins to stiffen slightly, 5 to 8 minutes with a whisk or 2 to 5 minutes with an electric mixer (not too long, or you'll make butter!).

SWEET AND SALTY CANDIED WALNUTS

Makes about 2 cups

you will need

Measuring cups, measuring spoons, baking sheet, parchment paper, chef's knife, small bowl, whisk, medium (9-inch or larger) nonstick skillet, wooden spoon

ingredients

1 sprig fresh rosemary

2 tablespoons superfine sugar

1/8 teaspoon coarse salt

1 cup shelled walnut pieces

1 tablespoon unsalted butter

preparation

1 Line a baking sheet with parchment paper.

2 Remove the leaves from the rosemary by holding the top of the stem with one hand while pinching it between the thumb and forefinger of your other hand and running them down the length. **Chop** the leaves finely (ant size; remember to use "the claw" to protect your fingers); you should have about 1 tablespoon.

3 In a small bowl, whisk together the sugar, salt, and chopped rosemary. Pour the walnuts onto a clean cutting board. If they are larger than halves, break them up into smaller pieces; a mix of halves and quarters is good.

4 In a medium nonstick skillet over low heat, melt the butter. Add the sugar mixture and then add the walnuts. Turn the heat to high and stir *the entire time* with a wooden spoon. The sugar will be in clumps at first. Keep stirring! Break up the clumps and move the walnuts around so they get coated.

5 After about 3 minutes, the sugar will begin to brown and **caramelize** (become sticky). Keep stirring so the walnuts are coated, then take the pan off the heat and turn off the stove. Use the wooden spoon to scrape the walnuts onto the prepared baking sheet and arrange them in a single layer. The candy will be *extremely* hot, so be careful not to touch it. Let the walnuts cool for 3 minutes before handling or serving.

6 Candied walnuts will keep in a tightly sealed container at room temperature for up to 2 weeks.

PEACH AND NECTARINE CRISP

Crisp gets its name from the butter and brown sugar topping that crisps up as it bakes, sealing in the heat so the fruit is steamed into a soft, syrupy jam. Any stone fruit—those jewels of summer that have a pit or "stone" in the middle, such as peaches, plums, and nectarines—will work well. Make crisps all year-round by substituting fruit in season, berries in spring and apples or pears in winter and fall.

you will need

Measuring cups, measuring spoons, paring knife, vegetable peeler, 2 medium bowls, wooden spoon, 9-inch glass or ceramic baking dish, whisk, oven mitt

ingredients

FOR THE FILLING

1 pound ripe yellow peaches

1 pound ripe yellow nectarines

1 tablespoon all-purpose flour

2 tablespoons granulated sugar

¼ cup blueberries (optional)

preparation

Make the filling

1 Slice off the top and bottom of the peaches; this will make them easier to peel. Using a vegetable peeler, carefully remove the skin from each peach. (The nectarines do not need to be peeled; their skin will cook nicely into the crisp.)

2 Place the peaches cut-side down on a cutting board. Use the paring knife to cut each peach in half and remove the pit. With the halves facedown, cut them into bite-size pieces. Prepare the nectarines the same way.

3 In a medium bowl, combine the flour, sugar, and fruit; add the blueberries (if using); and stir to mix with a wooden spoon.

4 Scrape the fruit mixture into a 9-inch glass or ceramic baking dish.

CONTINUED

FOR THE TOPPING

²/₃ cup all-purpose flour

²/₃ cup rolled oats

½ cup **packed** brown sugar

½ teaspoon ground cinnamon

A **pinch** of coarse salt

½ cup unsalted butter

Vanilla ice cream for serving

Make the topping

1 Position a rack in the middle of the oven and preheat the oven to 375°F

2 In a clean medium bowl, whisk together the flour, oats, brown sugar, cinnamon, and salt until you can see that the cinnamon has been completely mixed in.

3 Cut the butter into small pieces (¼-inch square, or about the size of your thumbnail) and add it to the flour mixture. With clean hands, massage the mixture gently until it just comes together like a loose dough.

4 Sprinkle all of the topping over the filling in a thin layer.

5 **Bake** on the middle rack until the filling is bubbling at the surface and the top is golden brown, 35 to 40 minutes. Remove from the oven (use an oven mitt), turn off the oven, and allow the crisp to cool for 5 minutes.

6 Spoon the crisp into bowls while it's still warm, and serve with a scoop of vanilla ice cream.

WHAT IS PACKED BROWN SUGAR?

To measure brown sugar correctly, it must be packed into a measuring cup. The easiest way to do this is to spoon the sugar into the cup and, with a clean and dry hand, gently press it down into the cup. Keep adding sugar and pressing until it's level with the amount called for in the recipe.

PIECE-OF-CAKE LEMON CAKE

In honor of my favorite fruit, here is an easy cake that stars lemons in all their mouthwatering, puckery glory. Olive oil takes the place of butter, which may sound weird but tastes great, and makes for an ultra-moist treat.

you will need

Measuring cups, measuring spoons, 9-inch round cake pan, parchment paper, medium bowl, zester, paring knife, small bowl, large bowl, small spoon, whisk, wooden spoon, toothpick, oven mitt

ingredients

1¼ cups all-purpose flour

½ teaspoon baking powder

¼ teaspoon baking soda

¼ teaspoon coarse salt

3 lemons

2 eggs

½ cup whole milk

¾ cup extra-virgin olive oil (see Note)

1¼ cups sugar

Fresh sliced strawberries for serving

preparation

1 Preheat the oven to 350°F. Line a 9-inch round cake pan with parchment paper so that the paper reaches just over the edges of the pan.

2 In a medium bowl, combine the flour, baking powder, baking soda, and salt and stir to mix.

3 Using a zester, **zest** one of the lemons. Cut the lemon in half, juice it into a small bowl, and remove any seeds. You will need ¼ cup juice; so juice the other lemons if needed.

4 In a large bowl, crack the eggs and remove any shell with a small spoon. Add the milk and whisk for no more than 1 minute, then add the olive oil, sugar, lemon zest, and lemon juice and stir well with a wooden spoon.

5 Add the dry ingredients (flour mixture) to the wet ingredients (milk mixture) all at once and stir until well combined. Pour the batter into the prepared cake pan.

6 **Bake** until the edges pull away from the sides of the pan, 40 to 45 minutes. To test, insert a toothpick into the center of the cake; if it comes out clean, the cake is ready. If there are crumbs attached, bake for a few more minutes and test again. Remove from the oven (use an oven mitt) and turn the oven off. Let the cake cool for 10 minutes, then move it to a plate by lifting up the parchment paper from both sides, or slice the cake right in the baking dish.

7 Serve warm with fresh sliced strawberries. Lemon cake will keep, wrapped tightly in plastic wrap at room temperature, up to overnight.

NOTE

For the best flavor, choose extra-virgin olive oil over "pure" or "light" olive oil. The "pure" oils are actually more processed than extra-virgin (also called cold-pressed) and may taste spicy or bitter.

The "lava" inside these cupcakes firms up as they cool down, so for the most ooey-gooey treat, serve them right out of the oven!

CHOCOLATE LAVA CUPCAKES

Imagine your dream cupcake, where a crumbly, brownie-like shell surrounds a chocolate lava flow in the center. That's this cake! For oozey, molten cupcakes, serve them right out of the oven. For firmer cupcakes that are more like the moistest-ever brownies, wait 10 minutes before you gobble them up. The best part? They take only 20 minutes or less, start to finish!

you will need

Measuring cups, measuring spoons, muffin pan, paper cup liners, medium bowl, whisk, small saucepan, wooden spoon, oven mitt, small spoon

ingredients

¼ cup sugar

2 eggs plus 2 egg yolks (see "How to Separate Eggs," page 158)

½ cup unsalted butter

¾ cup plus 1 tablespoon semisweet chocolate chips

2 teaspoons all-purpose flour

1 teaspoon unsweetened cocoa powder

A **pinch** of coarse salt

Vanilla Whipped Cream (page 148) and/or raspberries for **serving** (optional)

preparation

1   Preheat the oven to 450°F. Line a muffin pan with six paper cup liners.

2   In a medium bowl, combine the sugar, eggs, and egg yolks and **whip** with a whisk until the mixture is **frothy** and the sugar is dissolved, 1 to 2 minutes.

3   In a small saucepan over low heat, warm the butter until just melted. Remove the pan from the heat, turn off the stove, and stir in the chocolate chips until they are melted and smooth.

4   Pour the egg mixture into the chocolate and stir with a wooden spoon. Sprinkle in the flour, cocoa powder, and salt and stir again, until the flour is mixed in and the eggs and chocolate are blended—less than 1 minute. The batter should be thick like chocolate sauce. Fill each lined muffin cup with ¼ cup batter.

5   **Bake** until the cakes wiggle a little when you move the pan but aren't soupy, about 9 minutes. (If your oven runs hot, cook them for 8 minutes instead.) Remove the pan from the oven immediately (use an oven mitt) and then turn off the oven. Let the cakes cool for 3 minutes; they will be soft and gooey in the middle. To ensure they don't burst, gently remove them from the pan by sliding a small spoon underneath the cupcake liner and lifting out the cake, liner and all.

6   Crack open the crust and drop a heaping spoonful of whipped cream into the center, with a few fresh raspberries on top. Serve the lava cakes warm, right in the cupcake paper. Eat with a spoon!

HOW TO SEPARATE EGGS

1.

Wash your hands. Set out two small bowls. Crack an egg on the side of the first bowl and pour it into the bowl. Discard the shell.

2.

Gently pick up the yolk with your hand. Turn your hand palm-up, fingers just slightly apart, and let the white slip through your fingers into the bowl.

3.

Place the yolk in the other bowl.

If you're separating more than one egg, repeat the process, one egg at a time. This way, if you break a yolk, the whole batch won't be ruined.

TOOLS (THAT YOU WILL NEED TO USE THIS BOOK)

This may seem like a long list but I'm guessing you already have most of these things in your kitchen. You don't need to go out and buy special equipment to cook, but you do need a few basics like a knife and a cutting board. If the recipe asks for something you don't have, you might want to borrow from a neighbor or friend. And see page 7 for a refresher on knife skills.

SHARP TOOLS

Box Grater A four-sided grater with different-size openings on each side. Choose the large openings for grating cheese or carrots, and the smallest openings to zest citrus or grate hard cheese such as Parmesan. To use the box grater, hold the handle firmly with one hand, and grate the ingredient with the other, starting at the top of the grater and moving downward in one even stroke. Do not take your eyes off the grater—the holes are very sharp. Stop about $\frac{1}{2}$ inch before the end of whatever you're grating in order to protect fingers from getting cut.

Bread Knife A long serrated knife used for cutting bread, baked goods, and tomatoes. "Serrated" means the blade is jagged, not smooth, and has more "grip" on the food. Serrated knives are best for cutting tomatoes because the jagged edge can catch and break the smooth skin, while a smooth blade can slip.

Chef's Knife An all-purpose, straight-edged knife, usually 6 to 10 inches long, used for chopping, mincing, or thinly slicing virtually any food.

Handheld Grater A one-sided grater with a handle. Smaller openings make this perfect for zesting citrus or for grating hard foods, such as Parmesan cheese.

Paring Knife A short knife with a 2- to 4-inch blade, used for trimming vegetables and fruits.

Vegetable Peeler Peelers remove skins from vegetables like carrots, cucumbers, and potatoes. The stainless-steel blade can be very sharp. To use the peeler safely, hold it firmly by the handle and move the blade along the vegetable in one even stroke, away from your body. Hold the produce down on a cutting surface as you work.

OTHER TOOLS

Baking Dish A vessel used for cooking in the oven. Casseroles, lasagnas, desserts, and roasted meats and vegetables are usually cooked in a baking dish.

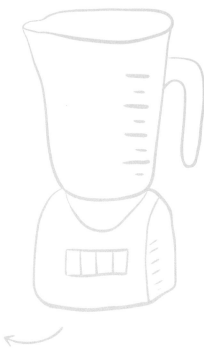

Baking Sheet A flat, rectangular metal pan for baking. Sometimes these pans have no sides and sometimes short sides (these are called rimmed). Good for baking or roasting cookies, pastries, vegetables, and meat.

Blender A tool with an electric motor and a rotating metal blade at the bottom for chopping and pureeing food.

Cheesecloth Thin, loosely woven cotton cloth, originally used for making and wrapping cheese, it can also be used for straining liquids.

Citrus Reamer A small tool with one or two heads for juicing all kinds of halved fruit. The larger head is good for lemons and the smaller one for limes. To use, place the head of the reamer against the cut side of the fruit, then push and twist. A fork also works for this!

Colander A bowl-shaped strainer with small holes, used for draining pasta and blanched vegetables or for rinsing fresh vegetables and fruit.

Cutting Board A wooden or plastic board for cutting vegetables, fruits, and other food items. For safety, always use a cutting board when using a knife; never cut on the counter.

Double Boiler A saucepan with two parts that fit together, one on top of the other, so the contents of the upper can be cooked or heated by boiling or simmering water in the one underneath.

Dry Measuring Cups Used to measure dry ingredients. They come in various sizes, like 1 cup, $1/2$ cup, $1/3$ cup, and $1/4$ cup.

Dutch Oven A large heavy cooking pot with a tight-fitting lid. They've been used for cooking, often over open fires, for hundreds of years. Good for long, slow simmering. The weight of the pot helps transmit heat evenly.

Electric Mixer (or Stand Mixer) A mixer that is either handheld with rotating beaters for light to medium jobs, or one with a more powerful motor that stands on the counter (stand mixer) and beats into a bowl for heavier mixing jobs, like kneading bread dough.

Food Processor Similar to a *blender* but comes with many different blades for chopping, slicing, mincing, grating, and pureeing a variety of foods.

Griddle A heavy, flat, iron pan, usually used on a stove, often for making pancakes.

Ladle A big scoop used to serve beverages, soups, stews, and beans, also great for pouring pancake and other batters.

Liquid Measuring Cup Used to measure liquids. The cup is clear and has measurements marked on the side.

Measuring Spoons A set of spoons for measuring liquid or dry ingredients; they come in different sizes, usually 1 tablespoon, 1 teaspoon, $1/2$ teaspoon, and $1/4$ teaspoon.

Mortar and Pestle A tool used since ancient times to grind herbs and spices and smash garlic. The mortar is the bowl and the pestle is the stick with a rounded end.

Oven Mitts These protect your hands from getting burned when inserting or removing things from the oven and removing hot pots from the stove.

Parchment Paper A moisture-resistant paper used to keep things from sticking when baking. Parchment can be used to line cake pans and baking sheets, or to roll out dough in place of a cutting board.

Pepper Grinder A small, handheld tool used to grind fresh black peppercorns.

Rolling Pin A cylindrical wooden tool used to flatten all types of dough.

Rubber Spatula A long-handled tool with a flat, rectangular end made of rubber or silicone, mostly used in baking. The flexible end makes it easy to scrape batter or dough from the bowl.

Salad Spinner A bowl-shaped tool used to wash and spin-dry greens. It consists of three parts, a bowl, a basket that sits inside the bowl, and a cover with a lever that makes the inner bowl spin.

Saucepan A tall, straight-sided pot with a small surface area to prevent evaporation. Good for soups, sauces, cooking food in liquids, heating liquids, and boiling eggs.

Small Saucepan: 1½ quarts. Good for heating liquids, reheating leftovers.

Medium Saucepan: 2 quarts. Good for small batches of soups and sauce.

Large Saucepan: 3 to 4 quarts. Good for soups, big batches of sauce, mashed potatoes, steaming and blanching vegetables.

Skillet (or Sauté Pan) A wide, shallow pan for sautéing, frying, and stir-frying.

Slotted Spoon Used for lifting vegetables, pastas, or grains out of liquid. The slots allow the liquid to drain away so only the food remains.

Spatula A long-handled tool with a flat, wide, rectangular end used to flip things without breaking them, such as fried eggs or pancakes.

Stockpot A large, tall pot that is taller than it is wide and comes with a lid. It's used to boil water for cooking pasta and vegetables, and also for simmering stocks, soups, stews, or sauces.

Strainer A bowl-shaped tool with holes for draining pasta and blanched vegetables, and rinsing fruit and vegetables.

Tongs A tool with two movable arms that is used to remove food (like corn on the cob) from hot water or a steamer basket, or to turn food (like sausages) on a barbecue.

Whisk A long-handled tool made of looped wires for blending ingredients, adding air to mixtures, and getting rid of lumps in sauces and gravies.

Wire Cooling Rack A rack for evenly cooling cookies, bread, and other baked things.

Wooden spoon A long-handled spoon used for mixing ingredients in cooking and baking. Especially useful when stirring hot foods because the wood doesn't get hot (won't transfer heat).

GLOSSARY OF COOKING TERMS

Airtight Sealed so that no air can get in or out.

Bake To cook with dry heat in a confined space (like an oven). Similar to *roast* (see entry), but most often at a lower temperature, 325°F to 350°F.

Blanched When ingredients are cooked in very salty boiling water for a short time, usually 30 seconds to 2 minutes, to preserve color and crispness. Some cooks transfer the food to a bowl of ice water to stop the food from cooking any further (common with green beans, peas, and asparagus). Blanched foods heat quickly, so they retain their color and texture as they lose excess water and firm up. Blanching also reduces the bitterness of greens and loosens skin, making things like potatoes and beets easier to peel. Blanch food in plenty of water with a 4-finger *pinch* of salt (approximately a heaping 1 tablespoon).

Blend To mix different things together until completely combined; can be done by hand or in a blender or food processor.

Blossom End The tip of the fruit or vegetable where a flower was produced.

Boil To cook quickly in briskly bubbling water. Boiling is used for foods that need to absorb water as they cook (for example, pasta) or for blanching vegetables (see *Blanched*). When the water is boiling, bubbles will erupt at the surface of the liquid and pop, letting steam escape. A rolling boil is when large bubbles erupt constantly, even when the liquid is stirred.

Caramelize To cook slowly (fruit or vegetables) until brown and sweet.

Chiffonade To slice very thinly into ribbons by stacking four or five leaves (usually refers to herbs, like basil or mint), tightly rolling them up *lengthwise* into a cigar shape, and slicing very thinly *crosswise*.

Chop To cut food into uneven pieces. A coarse chop means to cut into about bite-size pieces, and to finely chop means about ¼-inch pieces.

Compost A mixture of decayed organic matter used to fertilize soil, especially for growing crops. Compost is usually made by gathering plant matter (like leaves, grass, and produce) into a pile and allowing it to decompose. In cities that offer residential compost programs, compost is generally limited to produce but may also include meat and dairy products, newspaper and cardboard, and eco-friendly (biodegradable) plates and utensils, in addition to plant matter.

Crosswise When a recipe asks you to "cut crosswise," you will slice an ingredient across the short way. This is the opposite of *lengthwise* (see entry).

Dash A measurement of a very small amount of seasoning (such as hot sauce) added to food with a quick downward motion. It is between ⅟₁₆ and ⅛ of a teaspoon.

Dice To cut food into cubes. A small dice is about ¼ inch; a medium dice is about ½ inch; a large dice is about ¾ inch.

Drain To pour off liquid from food, like pouring cooked pasta and water into a colander. See also *Strain*.

Dust In cooking, "dust" is usually used as a verb, meaning to coat a cutting board or other work surface with a small amount of flour so that dough rolls out easily and doesn't stick to the cutting board.

Emulsion Two liquids that don't normally mix (like oil and water) combined by adding one to the other a little at time while mixing very quickly.

Florets The small, flower-shaped parts that make up a head of broccoli or cauliflower.

Frothy A foamy consistency; full or covered by a mass of small bubbles.

Garnish An edible decoration that finishes a recipe, like a chopped herb, grated cheese, or a sprinkle of cinnamon on a dessert.

Grease [verb] To rub butter or oil on a pan (like a muffin pan or cake pan) to keep food from sticking to it.

Julienne To cut (produce) into sticks like matchsticks. This technique is also used to cut vegetables into larger sticks, often called "batons," like french fries.

Knead To mix dough into a soft, uniform mass by pressing, folding, and pushing away from your body with your hands (or with a machine).

Lengthwise When a recipe asks you to cut "lengthwise," you will cut the long way. So if you're cutting a cucumber, cut all the way down the length of the vegetable (not across into rounds). See also *Crosswise*.

Mince To *chop* into teeny-tiny pieces, about the size of ants (the littlest ones). Mincing is even smaller than finely chopping. Used often for garlic, ginger, and herbs.

On the Bias When a recipe asks you to "cut on the bias," it means to cut at a diagonal angle rather than straight.

Ovenproof A pot or pan that can be used in the oven.

Oxidizing To lose freshness (for produce) and darken in color after prolonged exposure to air.

Packed To press an ingredient (like brown sugar or herbs) into a measuring cup. Ingredients can be tightly packed or loosely packed. For brown sugar, fill the measuring cup, press down with your palm or the back of a spoon, then fill and press again until you reach the top.

Pinch A small amount of a dry ingredient (salt, sugar, spices) that you can hold between the tips of your thumb and forefinger. It comes out to about $\frac{1}{16}$ teaspoon. A generous pinch is closer to $\frac{1}{8}$ teaspoon. Larger amounts, used for blanching and boiling, are sometimes referred to as a 3-finger pinch (roughly 1 teaspoon) or a 4-finger pinch (about 1 tablespoon).

Pith The bitter white layer between the skin and fruit of citrus.

Prep To prepare ingredients for cooking—for example, by cleaning, chopping, and measuring vegetables.

Repertoire The full range of what you can do. A chef's repertoire consists of all the dishes she or he can cook.

Reserve To set something aside for use later in the recipe.

Roast To cook in hot, dry heat in a confined space (like an oven). The heat should typically be 375°F or higher to brown the food. (At lower temperatures, it will *bake*.)

Sauté To cook fast over high heat on the stove until browned. Sautéing is good for meat and vegetables and usually requires some fat, such as oil or lard. When sautéing, make sure that the fat is hot but not burnt and that the food isn't crowded in the pan.

Savory Food that has a pleasant taste or smell and a spicy or salty quality without being sweet. The rich, round flavor of things like butter; it's also called "umami."

Set To become firm or more solid. Often used when cooking eggs. If a recipe says to "cook until the eggs are set," this means to cook until the eggs are no longer liquid but also not cooked all the way through.

Simmer A slightly lower heat than boiling, simmering usually requires a longer cooking time. A gentle simmer produces a few small bubbles every 2 to 3 seconds. A vigorous simmer has constant small bubbles breaking the surface with wisps of steam. The liquid and any added food flavor one another, so foods are often simmered in stock, wine, or other flavorful broths (like in a stew).

Steep To soak a dry ingredient (like tea leaves) in hot water until the water tastes like the ingredient.

Stem End The point of a fruit that was attached to the stem; it is opposite from the *blossom end*, where the flower was attached.

Strain To pour liquid through a strainer to remove seeds or other solid matter—for example, straining freshly squeezed fruit juice removes pulp and seeds. Straining is also used for custards and other foods to produce a smooth liquid. See also *Drain*.

To Taste When a recipe says season "to taste," it means add an amount of seasoning, like salt, spice, or vinegar, that tastes right to you.

To Cover When a recipe says add water "to cover," it means cover the ingredient with water; if it says "to cover by 2 inches," add water to the pot until it reaches 2 inches above the ingredient.

Well A hole at the center of dry ingredients (e.g. flour) usually made with a wooden spoon. Liquid ingredients are poured into the well and then mixed into the dry ingredients.

Whip To add air to an ingredient, like egg whites or cream, by beating it with a fork or whisk until it gets fluffy and light.

Zest The fruity outer layer of skin of a citrus fruit. Also the action of removing this layer (a recipe might say "Zest the lemon") with a peeler, grater, or zester.

ACKNOWLEDGMENTS

For Shelia, who disappeared into the refrigerator, with love.

Writing a book was so much harder than I thought it would be! I would never have been able to do it without my friends and family. Thanks first and foremost to Jasper and Romy for all of your feedback, patience, and excitement around this project and, most important, for being so much fun to eat with. You are my most proud accomplishment. I'm deeply grateful to my parents, Irwin and Ceppie Federman, for always being the most enthusiastic cheerleaders in the room.

There would be no book without Jenny Wapner, who agreed with me that kids are capable of anything. Thanks to Jenny and the whole Ten Speed team for their support of the project, to Ashley Lima for the clever design, to Aubrie Pick for the beautiful photographs, and to Matt Jervis for the sweet line drawings.

Thanks to the many chefs who contributed your creativity, knowledge, and recipes to this book and to the Charlie Cart curriculum. For recipe testing and so much knowledge and know-how, a huge thank-you to Chelsea Nichols, Amalia Marino, and Carri Wilkinson. For recipe development and laugh-a-minute moral support, thanks to my pals Siew Chinn Chin and Charlene Reis, two of the most generous people I know, and to my new friend George Dolese for double- and triple-checking everything and making it all look so good. The biggest thanks is to Alice Waters and the crew at Chez Panisse, past and present, for staying true to your beliefs. You are a sanctuary in this nutty world.

Eric, Alex, and Jaime, great work on the book title(s)!! And thanks for always having my back. You three are all better cooks than I am any day (especially Alex, if we're being honest). Mom would be proud of us.

For all other kinds of moral support, including eating the food and making me laugh, thank you to my smart and foxy friends Henni Yama, Sonia Fava, Joyce Cellars, Jill Martin, Daphne Beal, Seana Doherty, and Katrina Heron.

Most important, to the young people who so generously gave me their time to test these recipes and write up their feedback—good and bad—you have made your mark! This book includes all of your input, which you so thoughtfully conveyed to me. I am grateful to each and every one of you. A very special thanks to Arev Walker, who tested nearly every single recipe in the book with patience and moxie. My young recipe testers were:

Violet and Sam Bluestein
Elizabeth and Nicholas Bours
Ula and Elke Brucker
Calvin and Cora Day
Lila and Pablo De La Vega
Kalina Fairles
Ian Rock-Jones
Ella Kral
Jayshan and Arvin Parameswaran
Emmy and Davis Martin
Lulu Mead
Makenna and Caitlin Moore
Carla Fava Shmitt
Maia, Shea, and Aaron Stevens
Krithi De Souza
Knoa and Avi Tseng Jaffe

Our lovely and delightful chef/models were Jayshan, Arvin, Amar, Ella, Kalina, Ula, Grace, Gabe, Jaedyn, and Romy.

Last but never least, thanks to Noah Fairles, Nolan Darius, Jaedyn Tang, and Jasper, Romy, Juno, and Matt Jervis for happily eating leftovers with no questions asked.

INDEX

A

Agua de Sandia (Watermelon Refresher), 96

almonds
  Creamy Dreamy Almond
    Milk, 102–3
  Strawberry-Almond Milk
    Shake, 104

Apricot Quick Jam, 18

avocados
  Avocado Toast, 36
  opening, 38–39
  ripe, 36
  Summer Rolls with Peanut
    Sauce, 64–67
  Taco Party, 55
  Three-Minute Guacamole with
    Fresh Chips, 80–82

B

bananas
  Peanut Butter Power Shake, 70
  Strawberry-Almond Milk
    Shake, 104

basil
  Pesto, 49

beans
  Home-Cooked White Beans, 137
  as one of the Three Sisters, 85
  Taco Party, 55
  Two-Minute Green Beans, 125
  Warm and Cozy Sausage
    Soup, 134–35

beef
  Marble-Size Meatballs with Quick
    and Easy Tomato Sauce, 129–30

blueberries
  Blueberry-Lemon Scones, 14–15
  Peach and Nectarine Crisp, 150–53

bread
  Avocado Toast, 36

Marble-Size Meatballs with Quick
    and Easy Tomato Sauce, 129–30
Pan-Fried Flatbreads with
    Spiced Butter, 91–92
See also sandwiches

brown sugar
  Brown Sugar Butter, 19
  Brown Sugar Polenta, 22–23
  packed, 153

buckwheat flour, 26
  Pioneer Pancakes, 26–27

butter
  Brown Sugar Butter, 19
  Herb Butter, 19
  Homemade Butter, 19
  Maple Butter, 19
  Spiced Butter, 91

C

cabbage
  Curtido, 56

cakes
  Chocolate Lava Cupcakes, 157
  Piece-of-Cake Lemon
    Cake, 154–55

cardamom, 113

Cauliflower Poppers, Crispy, 87

Chai, Warm Masala, 111

cheese
  Cheddar Cheese Frittata, 30–32
  Chopped Greek Salad, 41
  Extra-Special Quesadillas, 51
  Ham and Egg Breakfast
    Sandwich, 24–25
  Marble-Size Meatballs with Quick
    and Easy Tomato Sauce, 129–30
  Melty Pesto Paninis, 49–50
  Spring Pasta with Butter Sauce, 46
  Taco Party, 55

Chicken, Crispy Skillet, 132

chickpeas, 78
  Thick and Creamy Homemade
    Hummus, 79

chiffonade, 8, 9

chocolate
  Chocolate Lava Cupcakes, 157
  Ice Cream Monday, 147–49
  Nearly Fudge Chocolate
    Sauce, 148
  Peanut Butter Power Shake, 70
  Perfect Hot Chocolate, 114

chopping, 8, 9

cinnamon, 112

citrus
  choosing juicy, 101
  peel, 99
  zest, 64
  See also individual fruits

cleaning up, 3

corn
  Fire-Roasted Corn On (or Off)
    the Cob, 83–85
  as one of the Three Sisters, 85

cornmeal
  Brown Sugar Polenta, 22–23
  Silver Dollar Johnnycakes, 28–29

Crisp, Peach and Nectarine, 150–53

cucumbers
  Chopped Greek Salad, 41
  Cucumber Salsa Fresca, 57
  peel, 74
  Summer Rolls with Peanut
    Sauce, 64–67
  Super-Simple Side Salad, 120
  Zesty Mango and Cucumber, 74

Cupcakes, Chocolate Lava, 157

Curtido, 56

D

desserts
  Chocolate Lava Cupcakes, 157
  Ice Cream Monday, 147–49

Peach and Nectarine Crisp, 150–53
Piece-of-Cake Lemon Cake, 154–55
Raspberry Clouds, 145
Tangerine Snow, 142
dicing, 8, 9, 138–39
dips
    Thick and Creamy Homemade
        Hummus, 79
    Three-Minute Guacamole with
        Fresh Chips, 80–82
drinks
    Creamy Dreamy Almond
        Milk, 102–3
    Mango Lassi, 107
    Mint Leaf Tea, 108
    Old-Fashioned Ginger Ale, 117
    Orange-Lemon-Lime Fizz, 99
    Peanut Butter Power Shake, 70
    Perfect Hot Chocolate, 114
    Sparkling Mint Limeade, 100
    Strawberry-Almond Milk
        Shake, 104
    Warm Masala Chai, 111
    Watermelon Refresher (Agua
        de Sandia), 96

E
eggs, 45
    Cheddar Cheese Frittata, 30–32
    cracking, 33
    Easy Egg Salad, 42
    Ham and Egg Breakfast
        Sandwich, 24–25
    Perfectly Hard-Boiled Eggs, 44
    separating, 158

F
Flatbreads, Pan-Fried, with Spiced
        Butter, 91–92
Fries, Sweet Potato, 88
Frittata, Cheddar Cheese, 30–32
fruits
    choosing, 4
    Fruit and Yogurt Parfaits, 13
    Honey-Cinnamon Granola, 20–21
    See also individual fruits

G
garlic
    burnt, 130
    Garlic Vinaigrette, 123
ginger, 113
    Old-Fashioned Ginger Ale, 117
Granola, Honey-Cinnamon, 20–21
Greek Salad, Chopped, 41
Guacamole, Three-Minute, with
        Fresh Chips, 80–82

H
Ham and Egg Breakfast Sandwich,
        24–25
herbs
    Herb Butter, 19
    spices vs., 111
    storing, 47
Honey-Cinnamon Granola, 20–21
Hummus, Thick and Creamy
        Homemade, 79

I
Ice Cream Monday, 147–49

J
Jam, Apricot Quick, 18
Johnnycakes, Silver Dollar, 28–29
julienne, 8, 9

K
knives, 7–8, 159

L
Lassi, Mango, 107
leftovers, 62
lemons
    Blueberry-Lemon Scones, 14–15
    Orange-Lemon-Lime Fizz, 99
    Piece-of-Cake Lemon Cake, 154–55
lettuce
    Super-Simple Side Salad, 120
    washing and drying, 121

limes
    Melon Wedges with Lime, 73
    Old-Fashioned Ginger Ale, 117
    Orange-Lemon-Lime Fizz, 99
    Sparkling Mint Limeade, 100
    Watermelon Refresher (Agua
        de Sandia), 96
    Zesty Mango and Cucumber, 74

M
mangoes
    cutting, 76–77
    Mango Lassi, 107
    ripe, 75
    Zesty Mango and Cucumber, 74
Maple Butter, 19
masa harina, 53
    Hand-Pressed Tortillas, 52–53
measuring, 6
Meatballs, Marble-Size, with Quick and
        Easy Tomato Sauce, 129–30
melons
    Melon Wedges with Lime, 73
    ripe, 73
    storing half, 72
    Watermelon Refresher (Agua
        de Sandia), 96
mincing, 8, 9
mint
    Mint Leaf Tea, 108
    Sparkling Mint Limeade, 100

N
Nectarine Crisp, Peach and, 150–53

O
oats
    Honey-Cinnamon Granola, 20–21
    Peach and Nectarine Crisp, 150–53
oil, 4
onions, dicing, 138–39
Orange-Lemon-Lime Fizz, 99

P

pancakes
    Pioneer Pancakes, 26–27
    Silver Dollar Johnnycakes, 28–29
Paninis, Melty Pesto, 49–50
Parfaits, Fruit and Yogurt, 13
pasta
    Spring Pasta with Butter Sauce, 46
    tips for, 46, 47
Peach and Nectarine Crisp, 150–53
peanut butter
    Peanut Butter Power Shake, 70
    Summer Rolls with Peanut
        Sauce, 64–67
pepper, 112
Pesto, 49
    Melty Pesto Paninis, 49–50
Polenta, Brown Sugar, 22–23
Potatoes, Salty Roasty, 126
preparation, 3

Q

Quesadillas, Extra-Special, 51

R

Raspberry Clouds, 145
recipes
    rating system for, 2
    reading, 1, 3
rice
    cooking, 63
    Sizzling Fried Rice, 60–63

S

safety, 2, 7
salads
    Chopped Greek Salad, 41
    Easy Egg Salad, 42
    Super-Simple Side Salad, 120
salsas. See sauces and salsas
salt, 4
sandwiches
    Easy Egg Salad, 42
    Ham and Egg Breakfast
        Sandwich, 24–25
    Melty Pesto Paninis, 49–50

sauces and salsas
    Cucumber Salsa Fresca, 57
    Nearly Fudge Chocolate Sauce, 148
    Peanut Sauce, 64
    Pesto, 49
    Quick and Easy Tomato Sauce, 131
    Strawberry Sauce, 17
Sausage Soup, Warm and Cozy, 134–35
Sautéed Things, 58
Scones, Blueberry-Lemon, 14–15
shakes
    Peanut Butter Power Shake, 70
    Strawberry-Almond Milk
        Shake, 104
Silver Dollar Johnnycakes, 28–29
smell, importance of, 50
Soup, Warm and Cozy Sausage, 134–35
spices, 4, 111, 112–13
spinach
    Cheddar Cheese Frittata, 30–32
Spring Pasta with Butter Sauce, 46
squash
    as one of the Three Sisters, 85
    Sautéed Things, 58
strawberries
    Piece-of-Cake Lemon Cake, 154–55
    Raspberry Clouds, 145
    Strawberry-Almond Milk
        Shake, 104
    Strawberry Sauce, 17
Summer Rolls with Peanut Sauce, 64–67
Sweet Potato Fries, 88

T

tacos
    Taco Party, 55
    toppings for, 56–58
Tangerine Snow, 142
tea
    Mint Leaf Tea, 108
    Warm Masala Chai, 111
Three Sisters, legend of, 85
tomatoes
    Chopped Greek Salad, 41
    Cucumber Salsa Fresca, 57
    Quick and Easy Tomato
        Sauce, 131

tools, 159–61
tortillas
    Extra-Special Quesadillas, 51
    Hand-Pressed Tortillas, 52–53
    Taco Party, 55
    Three-Minute Guacamole with
        Fresh Chips, 80–82

V

vanilla, 113
    Vanilla Whipped Cream, 148
vegetables, 4. See also individual
        vegetables
vinaigrettes, 122
    Basic Vinaigrette, 123
    Garlic Vinaigrette, 123

W

Walnuts, Sweet and Salty Candied, 149
Watermelon Refresher (Agua de
        Sandia), 96
Whipped Cream, Vanilla, 148

Y

yogurt
    Fruit and Yogurt Parfaits, 13
    Mango Lassi, 107

Z

zucchini
    Sautéed Things, 58

Published in the United States by Ten Speed Press, an imprint of the Crown
Publishing Group, a division of Penguin Random House LLC, New York.
www.crownpublishing.com
www.tenspeed.com

Ten Speed Press and the Ten Speed Press colophon are registered trademarks
of Penguin Random House LLC.

Library of Congress Cataloging-in-Publication Data:
    Names: Federman, Carolyn, author.
    Title: New favorites for new cooks : 50 delicious recipes for kids to make /
        Carolyn Federman.
    Description: First edition. | California : Ten Speed Press, [2018] | Age 8-18. |
        Includes bibliographical references and index.
    Identifiers: LCCN 2017040332 (print) | LCCN 2017047532 (ebook) | (hardcover
        : alk. paper)
        9780399579462 (eISBN)
    Subjects: LCSH: Cooking—Juvenile literature. | Youth—Nutrition—Juvenile
        literature. | LCGFT: Cookbooks.
    Classification: LCC TX652.5 (ebook) | LCC TX652.5 .F424 2018 (print) |
        DDC 641.5—dc23
    LC record available at https://lccn.loc.gov/2017040332

Hardcover ISBN: 978-0-399-57945-5
eBook ISBN: 978-0-399-57946-2

Printed in China

Design by Ashley Lima
Food styling by George Dolese
Food assistants Amy Hatwig and Elisabet DerNederlanden
Prop styling by Claire Mack

10 9 8 7 6 5 4 3 2 1

First Edition